CO₁₅

Sensei and his people

Sensei and his people

The Building of a Japanese Commune

Yoshie Sugihara
and
David W. Plath

University of California Press
Berkeley and Los Angeles
1969

University of California Press
Berkeley and Los Angeles, California
University of California Press, Ltd.
London, England
Copyright © 1969, by
The Regents of the University of California
Library of Congress Catalog Card Number: 69–15427
Printed in the United States of America
Designed by Dave Comstock

Ordinary life, extraordinary people

Sensei is one of those words that taunt a translator. Learning its dictionary definition is easy; learning its meaning in practice takes you far afield into the ideas, emotions and habits that make Japanese life recognizably Japanese.

Sensei is an everyday noun that denotes a teacher or master or spiritual leader. You find yourself using it frequently when you speak to or speak about a classroom instructor, a medical practitioner, a priest, or a professional artist or craftsman. But you also hear it being used out of respect and esteem for leaders of many kinds. Sometimes you hear it spoken ironically: "I'm not so stupid you need to call me sensei." But overwhelmingly you find that it connotes honor and devotion for a leader one knows and trusts deeply.

A non-Japanese can begin to comprehend this partly through abstract explanations. An American will readily think of parallels in his own attitudes toward doctors and priests and professors, although he has no single term like sensei that encompasses all of them. But short of actively living in a Japanese milieu, the alien can best come to appreciate the meaning of the concept by vicariously taking part in the life of a sensei and his followers. My main reason for preparing this book is to provide, in a small way, that kind of opportunity.

An institution, in Emerson's famous phrase, is the lengthened shadow of a man. These chapters introduce us to Ozaki Masutarō, the man and sensei, and to Shinkyō, the community which has grown in his shadow. Spurned by the Tenri church for heresy, ostracized by their home village, Ozaki and his followers went on to create a new community that has flourished despite years of hardship and pervasive opposition—perhaps, indeed, flourished because of it.

For an American counterpart one might recall John Humphrey Noyes and the development of his Oneida community in upstate New York, or some of the lesser known "backwoods utopias" of the nineteenth century. The social strains of modernization have stirred up secular communalist movements in both nations, though possibly to a lesser degree in Japan. The American examples have been much studied; the Japanese ones are virtually unknown. To this extent the book may have some novelty because it offers a detailed narrative of the development of one such Japanese group, as related by one of its leading members.

But if that were all, I am not sure the labor of translation would be worthwhile. The value of Mrs. Sugihara's narrative goes far beyond the depiction of Shinkyō as a communalist case-study. It gives us a front-row seat for scenes in the drama of Japanese life that otherwise we might never see. Americans in general probably know more today about Japan than any other country in Asia. In the last two decades several million Americans have lived there, and more than forty thousand have brought home Japanese spouses. Thousands of visitors from both countries cross the Pacific each year. Economically and politically we are most-favored-nations to each other. Things Japanese are featured in our mass media and art museums, and increasingly in our machinery salesrooms. For the more bookish, there are shelves of Japanese novels in English translation, and an endless flow of scholarly studies.

Yet despite it all, many of the more ordinary aspects of

Japanese life, as Japanese themselves feel and experience it, fail to come through. This is especially true of rural and working-class life. Even the novels, valuable as they are, tend to portray the middle and upper class urban ways the novelists know best. My fellow ethnographers and I have been struggling to make up for some of these deficiencies. We endeavor to be "participants" as well as observers, to report as well as human beings can the meaning of life as understood by an alien group we live among. Sometimes I think we are fairly successful at this. But even the best studies I know of still suffer from a certain "external" flavor—which may be inescapable to the extent that we remain outsiders and "observers" as well as erstwhile participants.

As ethnographers we take it as one of our duties to serve as spokesmen for the people we study: to see that their way of life receives a fair hearing in the domestic marketplace of human values. It is, after all, one of the few ways we can begin to repay our hosts. An ethnographer who has studied a non-literate tribe may be obliged to act as a kind of universal expert on and spokesman for "his" people; but it would be absurd and pretentious for him to attempt it for ninety million Japanese. There are enough regular Japanese "cultural ambassadors" who can effectively speak not only for governmental affairs but also for art, science, business and technology. In these circumstances the ethnographer's first task is to speak for the voiceless. This may mean in part that he reports on underprivileged classes and groups. It also means he must report "underprivileged facts" of many kinds that the cultural ambassadors choose to suppress or more often simply ignore as too commonplace.

These commonplaces—the imponderabilia of life, as Malinowski called them—remain grossly under-reported despite all our technological pride in instantaneous global high-fidelity stereophonic color television. The challenge is to make them exciting enough to be meaningful without making them seem so exotic they become mawkish. Narrative and biography long have been useful forms for this, and in recent years Oscar Lewis has been developing a family-history technique that affords a new format for ethnographic realism. For non-literate tribesmen or for "functionally illiterate" peasants and workers, an ethnographer may be obliged to create documents of this kind by using his tape recorder or taking dictation. Among a people as literate and as script-oriented as the Japanese he sometimes is lucky enough to find a good document readymade. This was how I felt when I first turned the pages of Mrs. Sugihara's narrative.

Ozaki and the Shinkyō people are not in some simple sense average or typical Japanese. But then they are not merely average human beings. This is what makes the narrative exciting. Their energy and doggedness, their solidarity and ability to overcome "amoral familism," would make them stand out, I believe, in any average group of humans. However, I believe that they can be usefully seen as *representative* in the same way and to the same extent that Oneida could be taken as representative of nineteenth-century America. That is, the overwhelming majority of their ideas and feelings and actions are ones that their countrymen would recognize as common sense. On a very few points they do run counter to what we might call "gross national custom." But the real difference is that they have taken a few of the same ideals to which most of their countrymen also aspire, and have managed to live them out more literally and thoroughly than the average man. The basic themes are the same; only the performance differs. Since Mrs. Sugihara wrote her book with gross national custom in mind, she is fairly explicit about where Shinkyō differs from it and in what ways. I believe that this will be readily apparent to a sensitive American reader.

The "farmer virtues" Mrs. Sugihara often speaks about are nothing peculiar to Shinkyō, and neither is the sense of trust in an intimate-yet-rugged paternalistic leader. These have been central to Japanese human ideals and ethical teachings for several generations. So the reader will learn about some very typical features of Japanese culture. But there is more. He will see how these features have inspired a community that is thoroughly mechanized and wholly of the modern world. If he is willing to see it as such, Shinkyō can provide him with a model by which to criticize the crasser claims of our conformitarian great-society mode of life. Ozaki himself would reject any such intellectual or ideological efforts. I do not and can not.

The first twelve chapters are my translation of Mrs. Sugihara's book, *Shinkyō Buraku*, published in Japanese by Shunjū-sha press, Tokyo, 1962. Mrs. Sugihara is Ozaki's common-law second wife, and has been his partner and companion throughout the building of Shinkyō. My translation omits most of two chapters of her text, and abridges several others. One of the chapters deals mainly with her personal affairs and adds little, I feel, to understanding Ozaki, Shinkyō, or even the authoress herself. The other is a description of daily life at Shinkyō in 1962. In attempting to translate it I found myself adding too many notes, some to explain customs unfamiliar to an American reader, others to update the description to conditions today. Most of these points are covered in my Afterword.

I have strived for a readable style that approximates her informal, almost conversational way of writing. This means that from time to time I have cut repetitions which may have been effective in Japanese but which, when translated literally, came through in my American language patterns sounding merely garrulous. I divided the chapters somewhat differently than did her Japanese editors, and in about a half dozen instances I shifted a few lines to another section of the narrative. Apart from that the order of presentation follows her text. She is reflecting on the events of many years, and her narrative does not always follow a strict time sequence. As a help to the reader—and without meaning to appear pedantic—I have included a reference table of dates for the major events she relates.

All along I have had to battle that peculiar affliction of translators known as footnote cancer. A number of times I lost, at points where Japanese custom differs enough that I felt the difference should be explained to an American reader. There I inserted comments into the text but set them off with [brackets]. Mrs. Sugihara now and again shifts from standard Japanese into her native Kansai dialect. I am not fluent in it, and those who are may find that I have misunderstood a point or two. However, I have heard most of the events of the narrative—indeed some of them numerous times—as told independently by Ozaki and others, and am satisfied that I have not seriously misconstrued them.

The line-and-wash drawings which grace these chapters were prepared for this English edition by Miss Mizota Kotoe, an instructor in the Tokyo Women's Art College, during a visit to Shinkyō in the summer of 1968. The drawings include views of Kasama and its environs, and of its guardian shrine which is mentioned in Chapters Six and Twelve; of Shinkyō's buildings and grounds; and of the Shinkyō people themselves as they work, bathe, and relax. My thanks to Miss Ohira Suzuko of the Far Eastern Library, University of Illinois, for persuading Miss Mizota to take on this assignment.

The map of Shinkyō and its environs, included in Chapter One, is the handiwork of Mr. James A. Bier, cartographer for the Department of Geography, University of Illinois. The photographs of Ozaki Sensei and Mrs. Sugihara, inserted in Chapter Two, are ones which I took in 1965.

Many others have helped me in this work. Ozaki and his people stand foremost on my list of debts; but I also must mention Professor Yamane Tsuneo of the Department of Family Sociology, Osaka City University, who introduced me to Shinkyō; and Mr. Nonoyama Hisaya, who proved himself a polymath while serving as my field assistant in 1965. To all of them may the book stand in tribute.

Realize that this is a partisan narrative. Those attuned to the *Rashomon* nature of truth may wish to hear how these events appeared to the eyes of Seki Iwazō, or the "evacuee woman," or Police Chief Yoshimura, or the ordinary villagers of Kasama. Lacking reports from them, we must rely upon internal evidence—the internal evidence of the text, and that provided by our own inner understanding of common human nature. If our authoress is partisan, she also is complex enough—even when like Ozaki Sensei she claims to be simple—that I believe the reader will know when she is being defensive, and will be able to allow for it. After all, she is not musing on the mists of truth; she is trying to account for a lifetime of action.

Contents

List of major dates and events

CHAPTER ONE

The white commune

White Communist Village is the name that radio, television and the newspapers have bestowed on our collective way of life. Does the name fit the facts or not? Actually we do not know and do not much care. For one thing, we are completely ignorant about communism. During the war we were carrying out a mild religious reform, and that gave us the incentive to organize collective management and communal living. It was not because we had any hard "line" or "ism"—we simply had to do it or we would not have been able to survive. We had to firm up our union of households in order to escape all sorts of oppression from the village power structure. If we had not, I think we would have been crushed completely. But the result of our actions was a totally unexpected outpouring of slander and demagoguery about how our attitudes were "communistic" and "red." Because we have disgusting memories of that period— enough to make us choke—even though we do not know what communism is, we get very uncomfortable when people start talking about communism-this and communism-that.

However, if people want to think that what makes our collective way of life special is some kind of white (rather than red) communism, that is all right with us. We will not object. But frankly we are a little surprised and embarrassed about what is said by many visitors and by the mass media: that we are somehow an extremely different and especially smoothly successful model of communal living.

The truth is that we have lived through these decades unaware, indifferent to appearances. All of our members are farmers or shopkeepers or ordinary people; there isn't one with high education or social standing. We are people who have no affection for theories or lofty scholarship and the like. It is simply that we have worked hard, we truly have worked hard. In that and that alone do we have self-confidence. There have been dark, painful years when it did not look as though we would survive if we did not work and work and work without quitting. If you say we "must have something," maybe it is the natural wisdom furnished unconsciously by this work-and-work-only way we have lived. At any rate, in the last few years a little surplus finally has developed, and from time to time our neighbors and the public have turned to take notice of us. And now, thanks to all sorts of wild publicity by the mass media, we are beset by an endless stream of visitors who come to inspect and investigate us. Among them have been groups who we felt used the excuse of research or inspection but who actually came to Shinkyō to sightsee or to have a picnic. I cannot say it isn't a nuisance, but we want our attitude to be that we will offer a simple welcome to anyone, in a spirit of "not rejecting those who come, not pursuing those who leave."

We ourselves try to be more aware than anybody else that the Shinkyō communal way of life is anything but perfect and has its share of weak points and shortcomings, and we never once have had the conceit to call it a "model." That is why when we hear excessive praise we are confused. Likewise, when we hear advice or criticism that makes sense, it hits home and we feel that we must correct the situation right away. However, it's easy to *say* "correct the situation," but we are a group of eighty people. It is more difficult than you might suppose. Even when we recognize perfectly well that something is defective, often as not there are circumstances and good reasons why it got that way.

Also, up to now we never once have tried to explain ourselves to the public, and people in general have too many
misunderstandings, misinterpretations and groundless fears
about the way Shinkyō operates. Sometimes it makes me
smile bitterly. To the extent that outsiders hold to their
subjective views—and they are free to think what they
want, it doesn't especially hurt anything—their misunderstandings and misjudgments are imported back into Shinkyō
via various routes, and begin to sow mistaken ideas in our
members' minds until the situation just cannot be left alone.
One of my motives for writing these chapters is not that
I have a scheme to propagandize somehow or other; but
rather it occurred to me that, if I set forth at least enough
of an explanation to clear up unnecessary misunderstandings, I could ward off the worry that our internal ties might
be disrupted by others' wild imaginings.

At present Shinkyō has about eighty members. The
majority are people who joined us after the war; their birth-
places and earlier experiences are many and varied, and
their ages differ. It is a thoroughly mixed company. That's
why you can count on two hands the people who know in
detail the real conditions under which the four families—
Ozaki, Yamanaka, Mitani and Imanishi—were obliged to
take up communal living in 1937 because they had been
ostracized by their village. Since somebody like me ordinarily is not interested in the old times, I grow careless and
assume that whoever I am talking to knows about them; and
the Shinkyō member-in-good-standing gives a look of
amazement and says, "Auntie, I didn't know about it. Was
Shinkyō like *that* in the old days?" Ah, of course. . . . I
catch myself being absentminded, and when I think it over,
I realize that already more than twenty-five years have
passed since the first steps of our communal life. Even
among the people of Kasama (which includes our Shinkyō
community) there probably are few who clearly recall the

3

situation then. So I suppose I should take it for granted that the majority of the members, who came here from Kagawa or Osaka after the war, don't know much about it.

The "creators" of this communal life, the four families (and myself, as a constant companion in their activities) are bit by bit growing old. So while we still can, we said, wouldn't it be good to put together some sort of record of what we have done? Certainly the younger members will tell us whether or not what we did and what we thought more than two decades ago still holds good for the postwar present. Of course, the idea is not at all to try to force our ways upon the present members. It's just that if we can get them to know the facts about how we thought and why we came to operate this way, then later, even after all of us old folk have died, it may help guide them. That's my second motive for writing.

Haibara is on the Kinki Nippon Railway more than an hour from Osaka and two hours from Nagoya. The area is a highland well above the Nara plain, and the train reaches it by snaking back and forth halfway up the mountainsides. If you go west from Haibara not quite four kilometers, you'll come to our Shinkyō hamlet. When you have passed through Yasuda, with its twenty-some houses, and are about to cross the line into Kasama, you are at Shinkyō. Along the township highway on one side is our *tatami* [rice-straw mat] factory and warehouse; and on the other side, on a slightly higher terrace ten meters above, is a two-story steel frame apartment building. That is our Shinkyō headquarters.

The scenery between Haibara and Shinkyō is purely rural, like that you can see anywhere in Japan. Wide paddies push up, tier after tier, to the hilltops; dike-paths divide them like a chessboard, combining intricately lengthwise and crosswise. The people moving about all are farmers with their tools. Cows can be seen here and there, and blue smoke rises thinly from the hills on the opposite side. Dur-

4

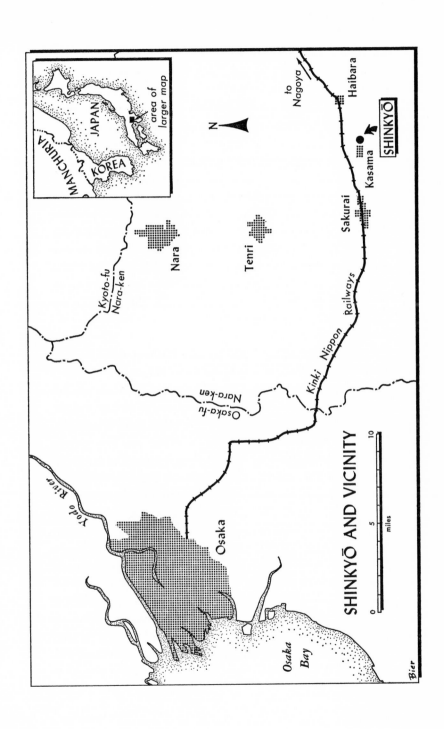

SHINKYŌ AND VICINITY

MANCHURIA
KOREA
JAPAN
area of larger map

to Nagoya
Haibara
SHINKYŌ
Kasama
Sakurai
Tenri
Nara

Kinki Nippon Railways

Kyoto-fu
Nara-ken

Osaka-fu
Nara-ken

Yodo River

Osaka

Osaka Bay

N

0   5   10
miles

Bier

ing the day while the children are in school there isn't a sound. The breeze that comes across the paddies is surprisingly cool. People who come to inspect us are surprised that in the midst of such a classic rural scene there is a building with big glass windows, green curtains, red roofs and white walls. "Just like a hotel, isn't it?" they say. And I suppose it does suggest some sort of Western-style mountain resort.

They say to us, "You've done all right to build such modern housing in these mountains. Whose idea was it?" Maybe they say this without malice, and yet somewhere in those words we sense an unspoken query, that "such a late-model apartment isn't appropriate to farmer status, is it?"; and we're stuck for an answer. If that were all, it would not matter; but most people add, "Seeing what a great building you've got, your mat manufacturing sure makes a tremendous profit, doesn't it?" And we more and more dislike talking to them. Isn't it *our* business whether we are trying to make money or lose it? True enough, speaking of profits, Shinkyō at the moment reckons a monthly cash surplus of a million yen [$2800]. But these profits are the result of the sweat and elbow-grease of eleven hours of heavy labor every day. We are not bothering anybody, and we are not depending on anybody's favor. And although we have a right to use our surplus any way we want, since we are not capitalists we don't need to accumulate capital, and we don't have any plans to make profits for ourselves by putting others to work and paying them wages. If there is money left, it is all right if we use it to put up new housing, take trips, or have new Western-style clothing made for everybody—whatever the members want and decide. At any rate, our idea is that profits made by communal living are best put right back into communal living, to make it more abundant and more convenient. That is why we do not intend to continue the eleven-hour working day forever; if possible we want to gradually reduce it. And there is no reason we should think we need to keep producing mats until eternity. For example, we talk about it every so often, and when enough people say they want to try dairying or fish-farming, we might possibly take that up, maybe in the near future.

Anyway, by nature we are farmers. We have confidence in hard work. That's how we stood up under several uncommon trials in the long interval up to now, so we have the stamina to endure most things. At the moment matters are going smoothly, but if there should be a depression in two or three years, I believe we would not groan even if Shinkyō's living conditions crack and take a sudden turn for the worse. When we remember the days right after the war, and how everybody's face turned yellow because we all were living on squash in order to save rice—a peculiar habit of rice farmers—we can be calm in any kind of poverty or pain.

But this kind of boastful storytelling could go on endlessly, so I had better get into the main topic. And as far as I'm concerned there is no other way to begin except by telling how it was that Ozaki Sensei and I became acquainted. Ozaki Masutarō is the spiritual pillar of our Shinkyō community, and is its leader in name as well as in fact. Without a doubt, if Ozaki Sensei had not been here, Shinkyō would not have started and certainly could not have continued. At present he holds several public offices, but Sensei still has a typical farmer personality. With a body that has endured sixty years, even now when 4:30 a.m. comes around he always gets into work clothes and goes to work with all the others. His face is sunburned and deeply furrowed; only his voice remains strong and youthful; the flesh around his shoulders and chest has grown terribly thin. No longer does he have the youthful face, bold and spirited, of that extraordinary Tenri missionary who ignored the utter poverty he was bathed in, and wholeheartedly preached his gospel. But then, when I count it up, that was more than thirty years ago. Naturally, both of us have accumulated wrinkles. And me, your authoress—well, at that time my tuberculosis had become critical. This body, which had been sentenced to die soon, had wasted away to nothing, a mere sixty-five pounds, just a pair of goggling eyes. What a difference from myself now! It was in 1928 that Sensei and I became acquainted, in Osaka. And so to begin I have to go back to 1928.

CHAPTER TWO
Encounters with Ozaki Sensei

My relationship with Ozaki Sensei has been constantly exposed to the eyes of the curious. He with a wife and children, me with a husband and son. When such a pair are always together, it probably is not strange for people to suspect some kind of immoral relationship. The villagers called us "red dogs in heat." When the police dragged us away for interrogations, they repeatedly asked vicious questions about it. But no matter how many times I tried to make them realize that they did not understand us, that it was their own lusting, the more I tried to explain the more they gave knowing looks and broad grins. Eventually I lost patience and made up my mind not to say anything else that might seem like an excuse. Some day they will understand the truth, I thought, and until then all I can do is grit my teeth and put up with it no matter how painful it is.

The damage went deep. Not only did spiteful gossip hurt Sensei and me, and the stability of Shinkyō; in 1943, shortly before the group migrated to Manchuria, Sensei and his wife, and my husband and I, finally had to be divorced. His wife and my husband gave as their reason that our marriages were totally unsuited to communal living. Although that was not necessarily just an excuse, the deeper reason probably was, after all, that the two of them did not have the strength to fight the persistent rumors that "Ozaki

9

Masutarō and Nishimura Yoshie are having an affair"; and so they yielded to it.

Anyway, the fact is that the thirty years also have included this tragedy, and in this sense it has been like struggling to live through a blizzard. So I think you will forgive me for humoring my feelings to some extent now as I look back.

In the fall of 1928 nobody, not even my family, seemed to think I had long to live, deeply consumptive as I was and caring for an infant. I became a more and more pitiful sight: down to sixty-five pounds, face-coloring blueblack, cheeks emaciated, only the eyes large. So bad that when I walked the streets everyone turned to look. The mild fever never subsided, and the bloody phlegm came out constantly.

Of course I was desperate and went around pounding on the gates of one doctor after another; but each gave no more than a vague opinion, and I couldn't believe any of them. Finally I saw one who said bluntly that of three advanced cases he was treating, of the same sex and age group, I probably would be the first to die and would be lucky to last another half year.

The Nishimuras—the family into which I had married —were pushing plans to divorce me from my husband and return me to my parents' house, on the grounds that it would be terrible if my baby became infected with tuberculosis. Although I was dimly aware of what they were saying, I was not particularly angry; on the contrary, I did not even think it unreasonable. Apart from the fact that I had no prospects for recovery, a true bride should leave a child after her if she dies. [In today's Japan neither custom nor law would uphold the Nishimuras' plan to return the authoress to her parents but retain her child, so she seems to feel obliged to defend them. At that time, however, both law and custom posited the continuity of the family line as an individual's highest duty. Parents were constrained to be responsible for their children's marriages. A bride who was married to the heir of a family line gained a husband, of course, but also "entered a house." Her first duty was to produce its future heir. To return her to her parents but keep her child might be painful, but it was proper.]

Truly I had neither time nor reason to let matters go on as they were. Like one drowning, I was clutching for straws. Given up by the doctors, all I could do was depend on the gods and buddhas: the power of religion. When I think about it now, I went through far too many church doors without getting any benefit. Even though the best I hoped for was peace and consolation and not a cure for my illness, none of the churches provided it.

Then late in the fall of 1928 a woman in the neighborhood gave me an introduction to a Tenri missionary. [Tenri is one of the oldest and strongest of Japan's modern-day "new religions." Founded in 1838 by a poor farmer's wife in the Yamato region around Nara City, not far from Kasama, it is the most popular and powerful church in that region today. Nationally it claims several million adherents.]

"If you think you've been cheated," said the woman, "by all means give him a try." Although I had no special hopes I went anyway, figuring "Why disregard a favor?" There really was just one thing that caught my interest: the character of this missionary Ozaki as this woman described him. She told me that her daughter of a few months had gotten a blade of grass stuck in her throat, couldn't breathe and seemed about to die. When the mother took the child on her shoulder, not to a doctor's but to Ozaki Sensei's place, he got the blade out and saved her. As the mother tearfully thanked him and said she owed him a life, he told her it was nonsense to say he had saved the girl. He said simply that while he had been running to a doctor's with the spent child on his back, the foreign object in her throat had become dislodged by itself; he refused to be made into a savior. The Tenri missionaries I ordinarily came across all were well-dressed, well-built gentlemen, clever talkers and pretty arrogant. Ozaki Sensei apparently was entirely different. And when I actually met him, he turned out to be a dark and husky boy, quite unpretentious, rugged in dress and bearing. In the way he spoke he had a farmer freshness pungent with the smell of the soil, and in his artlessness there was an honesty that made me feel I could trust him.

What did I talk to him about, that first time? I don't remember any more. It probably was not that deep or pointed a conversation. To me what was more important than anything was the joy of an overwhelming sensation that here was a religious man I could feel secure in contacting. I felt that in the darkness I had discovered the first ray of hope from that dim lamp I had so long sought and not found. With that I became completely unconcerned about how those around me looked at me or what gossip they exchanged about me; from the next day onward I began going to Ozaki Sensei's shabby little mission for daily services.

Of the things I heard from him in those days all I clearly recall is how again and again he stressed that in order to sever the roots of fate we must clean the dust from our hearts; specifically, we must do everything in our power to help others, without reward. Furthermore, he told me I must do everything for the sake of my husband who, because of my illness and other things, found me uninteresting. But more than for the content of what Sensei said, I was thankful that during the time I was with him I could at least live without thinking about my disease.

Were my family and friends disgusted by how much I had become absorbed with this church? They merely watched what I was doing with baffled faces; they said nothing, and before long the talk of divorce just faded away. Somehow or other my life, which had been given a limit of a few months, was saved. I didn't die; before I knew it my tuberculosis grew milder. Possibly it was chance. Probably it was a development that cannot be explained very well medically. But the unarguable fact is that I recovered.

12

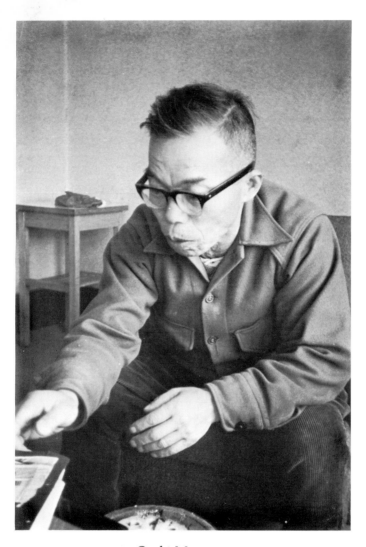

Ozaki Masutarō

Yoshie Sugihara

Who is this man called Ozaki Masutarō? Piecing together what I have heard at different times from Sensei himself with what I have heard from Yamanaka, Mitani, Imanishi and others, Sensei's early life was like this:

He was born on July 1, 1900, in Kasama, Asakura township, Kijō county, Nara prefecture. (Kasama now is incorporated into Haibara town, Uda county.) He was the third child, having an older brother and sister. His natal family was one of the leading farm families in a purely agricultural village; and it owned five acres of paddy, three-fourths of an acre of unirrigated fields, and seven and one-half acres of woodland. After he was graduated from higher primary school, he helped his elder brother on the family farm; but when he became twenty-one people urged him to enter the Tenri school at Tamba City. [Tamba City later was renamed Tenri City, as more befitting to the national headquarters of the Tenri Church. It is less than an hour's drive from Kasama.]

[While Ozaki was in primary school, his father died and his elder brother Ritarō became head of the household. Other sons had no claim to a share in the estate, under unitary inheritance laws then in effect; they were expected to establish new households of their own. Where farmland was scarce, as in long-settled Yamato, this usually meant that they must take up non-farm occupations. For this reason a family would attempt to send non-heir sons on for further schooling or training.]

Upon completing six months' training at Tamba City, Ozaki returned to Kasama and engaged in mission work at the Tenri chapel entrusted to his uncle Ōura Masujirō. In 1923 he went to do mission work in Hikone, Shiga prefecture; and after six months he went to what became his little mission at Tenkajaya in the Noda district of Osaka. In 1927, at the age of twenty-seven, he married a cousin, eventually becoming the father of a son and a daughter.

By that time he was personally responsible for his

Osaka mission, but unlike ordinary missionaries he would never take "donations" from his followers. As far as Sensei was concerned, a missionary who is a parasite on the faithful is a discredit to the faith and a source of corruption and decay. That is why he absolutely refused to urge the followers to contribute, insisting that his family would be completely self-supporting. He preached to his little band in a straightforward way, without flattery of any kind, what he himself believed. Therefore his mission utterly failed to flourish, and I suppose Tenri headquarters was justified from its point of view in scorning Sensei's mission for being unprofitable.

I have heard that once a member saw him carry a large board on his shoulder from Sennichimae to Tenkajaya while he was wearing the black kimono and skirt that are the missionary's uniform. The member was ashamed and said with a whine, "Sensei, at least refrain from behaving like that, please." But where Sensei was concerned, appearances and dignity did not matter. He was "scrubbed naked," as the saying goes; but he always held up his head, thrust out his chest, and defied public opinion. When I first met him in 1928, Sensei in those Tenkajaya mission days was right on the rock bottom of poverty.

One year, two, three . . . six years; they were gone before I knew it. I was caught up in one idea and one only: I wanted my disease to be cured. I wanted to be sure that I could forget my disease, and so I did not pay much attention to anything else. Of course a lot of things had happened both inside and outside of my family. With what strength I had, I struggled to serve my husband, as Sensei had told me, but I felt that conjugal love in the true sense of the term did not develop. More than a few times I thought we two probably should not have been married. Maybe we had what people call a "personality conflict"; anyway things just didn't go smoothly. My husband was bitter, I was dissatisfied. I do not feel like writing in detail about that situation, and since it isn't directly related to the main topic I would rather omit it. But I do need to record one thing. Every time I came up against anything difficult or unpleasant, Sensei never failed to be a good leader, good older brother, and heart's companion. I managed to survive by earnestly taking each and every one of his words as guidelines and as sources of moral support. Then one day when I happened to think about it I was astonished that a period of several years had flown by; I'm not pretending, that's really what I felt.

I don't know precisely when it started, but Sensei developed a habit of slipping away from us followers once a month and going back to Kasama. He made excuses about going to some church festival or a celebration at Tenri headquarters, but actually he was returning to his birthplace and diligently working as a farmer. He was very fond of farming (as he would reminisce to us now and then), and while living in Osaka away from the land he grew blindly in love with it. However, my guess is that his farm work was at the same time a side job, that it must have been a way to supplement his strained family budget. We believers were discontented about his trips. Once he had gone, he would not come back to his Osaka house (which was also his mission) for at least a week and sometimes for as long as half a month. So it became the usual practice for believers in the neighborhood to gather in front of a priestless altar, and with looks of mutual dissatisfaction conduct a service that completely failed to calm our ruffled feelings.

One day I asked his wife, "Don't you feel lonely when Sensei is away for a long time?"

She answered, "It's better when he's away. I feel more at ease."

I was a little surprised at her reply. Was she so confident about her husband's behavior, or was she resigned to the idea that nothing she said to him would matter?

Whichever it was, this was an unusual couple. Nevertheless, I envied them. When I reflect on it at times, I am ashamed; but perhaps it was because I was always bothered by how my own marriage was not going well. Anyway, even though I *was* close to the Ozakis, I had more interest than I should in the subtleties of their relationship and did not manage to hold back ill-mannered, prying questions.

"Sensei seems to be farming back home; how do you feel about that?"

"I hate farming and hate going back to the old village."

So that's it, I thought, and promptly closed in. "If you're willing to do it, I'll help you out as a maid or something—because I'd like you to go away from Sensei for a while. If you don't, we'll never get him to wake up."

Sure it's glorious to try to carry out your principles even though you are exhausted from shouldering demands you cannot hope to meet. But such a struggle is bound to end in failure. I mean that the result of his neglecting the mission and going to Kasama every month was that the mission's effectiveness could only go one way—down. I had no choice, I felt, but to be resolute about putting a hand in so as to force him to wake up and return to his calling as a religious man. I don't know what his wife felt deep in her heart as she listened to my suggestion, but from all I could tell she *seemed* eager to try it. If she went and lived apart from him for a while, Sensei inevitably would be driven to a position where he no longer could avoid making a decision.

At the time, Sensei was in the middle of talks with his friend Seki Iwazō in Kasama. Seki was trying to persuade him to return permanently. "The village hasn't got a single man with backbone who could be my counsellor; can't you come back and be my right-hand man in running this place?" Sensei by then was having grave doubts about missionary life, and he had come to the point where he struck against the fundamental issue: unless he went beyond the narrow frame of current Tenri doctrine, tangled as it was with a secular life and confusing worldliness, he could never achieve a true faith. He had trouble holding back the feeling that Seki's words were luring him on despite himself. Even though he did not agree with every aspect of Seki's proposal, Sensei returned to Osaka with his mind apparrently made up that sooner or later he would have to put an end to his missionary activities.

No plan his wife and I secretly tried to concoct would ever have meant much if Sensei decided he'd lost his enthusiasm for missionary life and wanted to step out of it. His other followers also lacked the power to persuade him to change his mind. When they considered the poverty his family had been living in for some years, which they very well knew, they were ashamed to be so cruel as to tell him he must give all his time to spreading the gospel. That was why we all went through a period of uncomfortable days— the way you feel when something's caught between your molars. This was in the late fall of 1935.

One day when I was visiting his house as usual, I blurted out, "Sensei, you know maybe Masako-san is near-sighted."

Masako was his daughter, age seven. After her came a son Shunji, age three. Lately we had begun to see funny things in Masako's actions and attitudes, but though we thought it odd we just let it go. I had been wondering for some time if it might possibly be because the child had bad eyes, which was why that popped out of my mouth. Sensei and his wife apparently had not given it a thought, so next morning in a rush he led Masako-chan to the ophthalmologist at University Hospital. ["San" is the everyday suffix title of polite address or reference, loosely equivalent to the English terms miss or mister or mistress. "Chan" is a more familiar and diminutive form used especially for children.] That evening a crushed Sensei came to my house holding Masako-chan by the hand. Tears glistened in his eyes. With a look on his face that made one wonder how a man could get so haggard in only a day, he told me haltingly the outcome of the examination.

"She's already nearly blind. The doctor said she might as well be put in a school for the blind."

The last was said with sobs. It hurt me to listen. His wife must be worried.

"I can't talk about it with my wife. She wouldn't know how to calm these wild feelings I have; she'd be more upset than I am and the two of us would end up going crazy together. That's why I wanted to come here first and talk to you."

For me it was a blow to hear that Masako-chan was practically blind, and a sad surprise to learn how Sensei and his wife were getting along. Here for the seven or eight years since I'd been married, I had had nothing but envy for the way other couples around me got along, and I had especially been jealous of Sensei and his wife; so this was something I hadn't expected to hear.

Refusing to accept the verdict, Sensei went off the next day to the ophthalmologist at the Red Cross Hospital; but the result was the same. The day after that again he called on specialists but he received the same answer.

Sensei grew bitterly discouraged; day by day I could see him wearing down. And once a day without fail he came to my house leading Masako-chan by the hand, never saying much, going away again sadly. On the rare times when he didn't come, I made a point of going to his place. His wife was crying her eyes red every day.

In this situation where Sensei and his family had given up hope and couldn't get a grip on anything, we followers were struck by a sort of gloomy unrest that went beyond mere sympathy. Especially me as the one closest to his family. Once I would think about Masako-chan, I couldn't settle down; many times—sometimes at three in the morning or around daybreak—I'd stand in front of his house straining to hear sounds from inside. If a stranger had seen me he probably would have thought I was a thief. But Sensei could tell the sound of my footsteps no matter how soft they were, at any hour of the day, and he'd call from inside, "Nishimura-san?" For many days now he too had not been able to sleep at night as he went on worrying.

"I was thinking that a little more of this and the whole family might as well kill themselves—then I heard your footsteps." He would say things like that. He could not forget about eyes even for a minute.

"All the neighborhood kids Masako's age went off to school again today with their bags on their backs. I can't stand watching them."

"I wish she'd slip and fall into the toilet and die. Just when I'm thinking what a blessing that would be, I see her walking to the toilet with her stumbling steps, and despite myself I race after her and hold her up."

"The feelings of a parent who has a crippled child are very complicated. I can't tell one thing from another anymore."

This from Sensei, who long had paid no attention to name, position, or property; who had sacrificed his family's well-being and found his reason for living in his faith. Furthermore, out of great fondness for his children he exposed them to severe training—from the time they were born he never once bought them a piece of candy. That may seem like a curious way to show it, but a parent's love for a child is something special.

As everyone with faith in his heart knows, the essence of a religious life is that when you are in trouble you discover joy amid your pains and can go on enduring them. Obviously a man like Sensei was aware of this; in fact it wasn't unusual for him to speak of it himself. But when Masako-chan's condition hit him Sensei apparently began to lose confidence in his faith and his mission. Or maybe more than anything it was that he was wandering in the dilemmas of any ordinary man, being burned in the flames of parental love and laying open exactly the same contradictory feelings of agony, grief and bitterness that other people have.

We thought Masako-chan only had bad eyes, but in fact that wasn't all. One day she suddenly began to have convulsions. At first they came only about once a month, then two times and three times, and before long she had severe spasms almost every day. Of course she was examined by the appropriate medical specialists, but they didn't know what caused it. The spasms grew worse and worse. She already seemed to have lost her mind. The look on her face was plainly different from the one she used to have.

Little by little Sensei grew nearer to being resigned to it. But this was definitely not because of understanding or insight, as I could tell from the many times he'd let slip phrases like, "It would be better for this child to die soon."

As for myself, whenever I saw Sensei in such a pitiful state I could not calm my upset feelings. I mean, doubts about my own faith began to rear up. Nine years already had gone by since I first knew Sensei as a missionary of twenty-eight. I lived those years in gasps, struggling against disease, starving for a husband's love. I would have broken to bits physically and mentally long ago if I had not had Sensei. But now that much-needed Sensei was being attacked by his child's calamity and was so much in pain— that bright-hearted Sensei who almost never thought of himself. Rewards of charity? Retributions of karma? Aren't they just tales told by idiots? Why doesn't this Sensei please the hearts of the gods? Can there really be gods so merciless?

In my case there were. Of the many things I prayed for I don't think one was granted, except that this body which people were skeptical about still was living. But the heart had not been saved. Even though she is poor, even though she is sick, a wife's greatest treasure is a husband's love; but although I had continued to seek it for these nine years, I was not able to find it. Was my faith useless too, then?

Eventually I took to bed. After I had thought about it in bed for a few days, I struggled to my own conclusion. It was this:

Yes, up to now I had been seeking desperately. And I had come to think that "faith" meant praying fervently to the gods. Once in a while I'd had my heart examined by this nearby Sensei. However, he is now perplexed by his child's illness, and he wants to farm at his home village, but he has not been able to make up his mind. Change pain into joy, they say, draw closer and closer to the gods no matter what your trouble, in fact because of your trouble. . . . This is big talk, but isn't it brought on by our pride? Does anything happen when we are impatient to force the will of the gods to bend in our favor?

Suddenly I didn't worry about poverty anymore. If I got sick, it would be all right to recover and all right not to; it would be good to have a husband's love and good not to; all right to die and all right to live . . . leave everything to the will of the gods. . . .

Once I had gone into this state of mind I finally was able to get out of bed. And my reward was that I had become buoyant, like a fool or a spark, and had the feeling that I had left behind me all desire for love, fame or goods. Whatever happened would be fine with me.

When I went to see how things were at Sensei's house for the first time in a while, I found Sensei as before, sullen, with a dark expression on his face. And when Masako-chan raised her vacant eyes and looked up at me, the expression on her face was almost completely moronic. Obviously the disease that was ruining her mind had progressed steadily in the brief time I hadn't seen her. In fact, as I was watching her face an idea that had occurred to me in bed, and which I had quickly snuffed out, suddenly jelled into a resolve. Yes, no doubt this was the very best way. That is, to be blunt about it, I thought I would go together with Masako-chan on the death journey. It would repay my debt to Sensei for having so long helped me, and maybe Masako-chan herself would forgive me.

So one day when I was leaving Sensei's house after a casual visit, I said blandly, "I'll have Masako-chan sleep at my place tonight, so don't worry." And without giving her parents any time to say yes or no I led her out.

"You'll die with Auntie so we can get rid of your father's sadness for him, won't you?" You could not expect an almost moronic child to understand, no matter how many times you said it, but I felt I had to lull my partner whose eyelids already were getting heavy from having played all day. Before I knew it I was looking into the sleeping face of a child who had begun to breathe easily. I would look at my hands, stand, sit; and just when I'd be about to act, bits of completely unrelated past experiences would suddenly pop into my head, and I simply could not go through with it. It seems strange now, that I was so tempted and so indecisive; but nothing happened after all. However I never once thought it was evil. Far from it, I even thought it was beautiful.

The result was that dawn came as I was getting weary of wavering between choices. The bright morning light hurt my eyes. It seldom happened early in the morning, but there was a gentle voice at the entry. When I went out to see who it was, I found Ozaki Sensei. Apparently he had felt uneasy for some reason, and as soon as dawn broke he had hurried over to my house.

I thought that since it had come to this I didn't need to keep it a secret forever, so I confessed to him every single thing I had been feeling during that nightmarish night. Sensei blanched for a time. He seemed shocked to the core. We were silent a while, then at last he spoke.

"No, I did wrong. Right now I don't feel like criticizing your idea as being good or bad; I'm not the right person for that. I'm only thinking how sorry I am. Up to now I thought I might do away with the child, and even said I would, but when it came down to it I was just complaining. If you tell me I became a slave to my own complaints and forgot about more important things, there's nothing I can say. No, from now on I've got to think it out again. I'm the butt end of a man of faith."

As I heard what he said, the gloom that long had been lumped in my breast seemed to melt away little by little. In the end, I did not offer one word of apology to him for having planned to lay my hands on Masako-chan.

I do not think it can be helped if—depending on how you look at it—you say my conduct had a touch of madness. I don't deny it was out of the ordinary. Yet in passing through this crisis I discovered some sense of worth in me; and Sensei too seemed to have the scales taken from his eyes, and somewhere or other in his actions there was a new vitality. Before long he began to move from this religious turning point toward what we at Shinkyō call "the altar-smashing."

CHAPTER THREE
We smash altars

Sensei had long been opposed to the keeping of an altar in the house of a Tenri missionary. His argument was that the altar is a weapon by which the missionary extorts goods and money from believers, that it is nothing more than a means of life for the missionary and has no connection with saving the faithful. Of course, from the viewpoint of Tenri headquarters this idea unquestionably was fearful heresy, so that church leaders had no affection for Sensei and were downright unpleasant about his views. The fact that his beloved daughter was hideously diseased became the topic of topics for castigating him. "Heaven's punishment has struck." "It's your reward for not having believed more zealously and won more converts." "If you don't strive harder for the gods, the child's disease will not be cured." And so on.

But Sensei didn't have any expectations that his child would be rescued from disease in return for his striving or collecting converts. Not only that; he said, "A Tenri priest makes his living by hanging out a shingle that says All Diseases Cured. But if there is nothing I can do for my own child's disease, then the sign must be a fake. It is better to take down a sign like that." I don't understand difficult points of dogma, but Sensei's attitude seems to have been that if an altar becomes just a barrier to enlightenment in true faith, the gods who are worshipped at such an altar do not amount to much; so we should live by a spirit of faith in things-as-they-are or in the laws of the universe instead of such gods.

Sensei puts practice before preaching. He is a man who can't sit quietly and hide something which is troubling him. One day soon after Masako-chan's night with me, he cleansed his body with an ablution, and then before the eyes of a small number of followers he took down the altar of his own mission. This was the first "altar-smashing." The altar in my house came next. Then Sensei went around to the homes of each of the followers in turn, explaining why it was necessary to get rid of the altar; and if they were willing he took it down right then. Of course since they'd already heard about it, the idea wasn't new to their ears. But "followers" include all kinds of people. Those who had entered the faith out of admiration for Sensei's character were quick to agree with him, but those with a strong desire to worship idols turned and separated from him. People from Tenri headquarters said they had been expecting it, and they mocked him. "Rebel against the gods and you'll soon get divine punishment." One of his missionary friends needled him, "Aren't you using your child as a pretext for hoisting your own flag?" and thereafter broke off their relations. His younger brother, who had been on good terms with him, said, "You're upset because of your child," and stopped coming around; another younger brother said "The gods have possessed you," and began to keep a respectful distance. Around Sensei things suddenly had gotten lonely.

The new year dawned. A heavy snow continued to fall from the end of December into the New Year. I was invited along with Sensei when he returned again to Kasama, and visited this little mountain community for the first time. Day after day it was so cold there I felt naked.

Many Kasama people had been friends with Sensei since primary-school days. Four of them—his own older brother Ritarō, Yamanaka Hisajirō, Imanishi Tokuichi, and Mitani Sei'ichi—were not merely close to him, they were devoted to him as ardent Tenri believers. The members of these four families had been instructed by him on many matters of faith before this, and some of them showed unusual interest in hearing about the altar-smashing he had carried on in Osaka, inviting him over time and again to listen to his explanation and learn about his state of mind. He took their questioning graciously even though he had not encouraged it, and earnestly discussed everything in his usual unadorned way. He being a man they had trusted for a long time, the four families immediately supported him.

Under the winter sky the four families went around every day to homes of relatives and friends to wash away the past with a sprinkling of water. The idea was to receive forgiveness for harm done unintentionally, even though neither side was aware of anything wrong. Water sprinkling soon spread rapidly. About two-thirds of the people of Kasama were Tenri believers. The ripple that spread among them resulted in more enthusiasm than anybody had expected, and naturally enough there soon began to be excesses. Some people even came out and said, "Look! This time a blessed god has appeared. It's not like Tenri; you'll be saved even without offering money if you just sprinkle water and devote your life to him." When it got to the point where people were sprinkling water at random—as though sprinkling alone was enough—it was almost comic. But we were in no position to scold them for the way they were paying visits, like crows imitating cormorants.

On the other hand there also were people who tried to maintain the stand of the traditional Tenri believer, that "Even if your heart isn't penitent you'll be saved as long as you worship the gods. Above all, what's important is serving and progressing." "Serving" is giving wealth to the church, "progressing" is worshipping at the church. Of course, when you worship you must not go empty-handed. You have to take some goods along. Because they are taught that those who don't serve and those who don't progress not only lack divine protection but get divine "repairs" (that is, punishment by disaster or incurable disease), believers think half in fear and half in faith that progressive service is the core of religion. To wake people up from this drowsy faith one can't get by with halfhearted methods. Bold steps are absolutely essential. So Sensei began to feel more and more strongly that he should perform an altar-smashing in Kasama as he had in Osaka. Even so, I sensed that he was very reluctant at first. Perhaps he realized that since he was tied to the people of the village by an extremely complex web of interests, and since the Chief of the Tenri Chapel was a close relative, it would not go as easily as in Osaka where, like a real sensei, he was surrounded by a few followers and many strangers. However, water sprinkling had spread from the four families all across Kasama and into neighboring Yasuda; with the whole village now stirred up like a hornets' nest he no longer could ignore the situation. It goes without saying that a man like Sensei would be ashamed of that kind of cowardly, defensive conduct. So it appeared as though Sensei was being goaded by those around him in such a way that the matter would never end until he smashed the altar.

Ozaki Sensei was thirty-six, Ritarō forty-two, Yamanaka and Imanishi thirty-seven, and Mitani the youngest at twenty-eight; all were men of mature judgment. They weren't driven by hot-blooded passion like inexperienced boys, and they had the ability to carry something through once they had agreed on it. The four of them agreed with Sensei to smash the altar, and secretly swore their loyalty.

His uncle, the Chapel Chief, was their next objective. Since he was a man with many years' experience, they had to proceed very differently than they would with an ordinary believer. First, they launched a powerful flank attack. That is, the four men went to the Chief one after another, and with sharp words they prodded him to support Sensei's views. After all, these men were among the most powerful parishioners of his church; so because he was deeply indebted to them for supporting its activities up to now, the

Chief was in a dilemma and could not bluntly reject their request.

Then Sensei himself opened fire. Sensei didn't say that progressive service fails to reveal anything about a man's faith. If there are gods, surely they approve of the feeling a man has when he has left material desires behind. The problem is what to do about the goods offered to the gods. Sensei would say, "Offerings are the same as leftovers after the gods have taken their share," and have the believers take them back. He believed that it was even more outrageous to be living in worldly comfort while being supported by the faithful. The Chief happened to have four children, and the two oldest girls were going to girls' high school. In Kasama a family was considered pretty well off if it could send not just one but two children to school. Sensei began by jabbing away on this point.

"Chief, isn't the chapel being supported by the parishioners' sweat and hard labor? Seeing that some of those parishioners who are doing progressive service with their mites are hard pressed just to send their kids to primary school, it's preposterous for a priest to be so indifferent about it that he can send his own children to girls' school while he lives on other people's money."

Struck in a sore spot, even the smooth-talking priest was at a loss for words. He mumbled to himself that contrary to appearances he actually was dirt poor, and it really would not be right to make the girls quit school now, would it, when they had been going every day?

Sensei confronted him. "No, don't say you can't do anything about it any more. If it's what you want, you can at least become a handyman for the parishioners and go give them help with daily farm chores. You ought to be able to do at least that much. Ever since I realized that a priest is a faker I have tried not to earn my bread by cheating believers. Uncle, it's not fair to the faithful for us to be drinking tea and loafing every day, prostituting our words for our keep."

Charged in this way, the Chief had nothing to say. Besides, what Sensei was telling him was the unadulterated truth. Having forced him this far, Sensei slowly began to explain his own views. "Uncle, *because* you've got this altar you try to make it provide for you; and the believers on their part think if only they bow to it they'll be saved, if only they give progressive service they'll be saved. The source of all your trouble is this altar. Chief—Uncle—now's the time to make yourself into a new man and live like a true priest. If you really want to help people, don't you think it is a nuisance to have an altar?"

Sensei explained it over and over at slow speed, gently and calmly without getting angry. The Chief knew very well that Sensei was not telling lies or nonsense. And that was why he was trapped. He could not simply call it a pack of lies. But if he agreed with what Sensei said, he would have to carry it out. Unable to reject it, unable to admit it, he buried his head in his arms.

Because it was a real problem, rumors spread immediately; and there was great unrest among parishioners in Kasama and Yasuda. So the Chief could not let things be. He gathered a few leading parishioners in the chapel with the idea of asking them whether he should call a mass meeting of the faithful and get their reactions. It was at this session that Sensei first gave a public explanation why it was necessary to abolish altars.

Sensei came right to the point. "I tell you all that since the Church urges us to make offerings to the gods only because this altar is here, we need to smash this altar."

Building on his own experiences in Osaka, he talked about conditions in the Tenri Church and about what true faith is, in a way that soaked into our beings. It was not that he raised his voice or made grand gestures; a real sensei can be eloquent even when he's awkward. The main point of Sensei's argument—that it actually helps one's faith not to have an altar—was something anybody could agree with, and the majority of believers gathered there seemed deeply impressed with how reasonable it sounded. Also it was a situation they could correct by themselves. That is, the ordinary not-so-well-off parishioners there didn't have much reason to be happy about offering goods and money to the Church. But they would not have to worry about being squeezed by the Church if they took away its altar, so they concluded, "If that's the case, it's right to smash the altar."

But even though they thought so, they still were worried. Minds indoctrinated with the idea that the altar is the window through which you contact the gods won't easily decide to quit using that altar after they have heard the words of only one missionary. "Won't the gods' punishment strike us?" Their timid whispers to each other reached Sensei's ear. He spoke up at once. "I'm the one who suggested we smash the altar, and since I'll take the blame on myself, you can rest assured. Let's try it and see whether punishment strikes or not." I suppose it came through to everybody that Sensei was concealing powerful self-confidence under this banter. From that point on, their stiff faces gradually relaxed, a friendly conversational atmosphere developed, and the discussion began to move ahead smoothly.

This certainly was no issue that could be settled in one session. It was argued and re-argued for two or three days. It went on until all the views had been given that should have been given. The result was that, though I doubt that every single believer agreed to it, at any rate they accepted Sensei's proposal. And judging from their conversations, they seemed to have come to realize that at least it was not as fearful an act as they might have imagined from the gossip. Since this was the general will of his parishioners, by and large, the Chief was obliged to lend a hand in the proceedings.

The chapel was elegantly carpeted with twenty tatami, and the sanctuary was in the front of it. The biggest altar was about one and one-half meters wide and two meters high; on each side of it was a small altar, one said to be dedicated to the ancestors and the other to the foundress of Tenri. Although the altars were to be smashed, desecrating the spirits of the gods and ancestors was not the object, so Sensei asked the Chief to take down the sacred objects.

Well, the time finally came. The village faithful were holding their breaths and watching the fearful sight intently. The Chief washed out his mouth, cleansed his hands, put on a mask, and took the sacred objects away. The altar-smashing itself was carried out by the four families, as leading parishioners. You can call it an "altar," but if it has no sacred objects it is nothing but boards. In what may or may not have taken twenty minutes, the three altars were very easily broken up and neatly cleared away. It was much too unsatisfying a way to draw the curtain on an uproar that had involved so much wrangling. But the believers' faces showed they'd been released from tension, and they went home in threes and fives chattering quietly about one thing and another.

The smashed altar gave us plenty of boards and sticks. To throw them away would have been foolish. Sensei said we should heat the bath, so the wood immediately was made into kindling for firing up the chapel bath. Even so, nobody volunteered to get in when the water was hot. Sensei said, "What's the matter? Still afraid of divine punishment? If that's it, I'll go first." He stripped naked right away. When the four families heard him say cheerfully "Ah, it's great!," they felt secure for the first time and took baths one after another. Obviously punishment did not strike them.

CHAPTER FOUR
The village leaders react

The altar-smashing certainly did not end there; it stirred up an array of after-effects we could never have anticipated. And the greatest of all was the discord and conflict between Ozaki Sensei and the biggest boss in Kasama, Seki Iwazō.

Seki and Sensei had been childhood friends. Every time Sensei went back to Kasama from Osaka, he would get together with Seki and they would talk about anything and everything. When Seki came to Osaka and had Sensei help him buy a truck or a cow, he would stay in Sensei's house. I had a chance to meet him some of those times, when I went to Sensei's place for church services. Seki was full of self-confidence, and there was a streak of pride and deceit in him; he did not make a very good impression on me.

Kasama has about seventy households; Seki, as holder of seven different community offices—village councillor, township representative, co-op leader, etc.—naturally was the most powerful man in the hamlet. Furthermore that power had come down from his father, and to put it bluntly his family had the highest "name" in the village. Therefore nobody would openly oppose him, and nothing he suggested would fail to be carried. A man in this situation is sure to become dictatorial and self-indulgent. It was said that even

Seki's relatives were timid and nervous when they came before him.

I never knew Seki Iwazō very well, but by an odd chance I developed a more-than-casual acquaintance with his younger brother-in-law Seki Kōsaku. Like Iwazō's house, Kōsaku's was located in the central section of Kasama, halfway up the hillside; but Iwazo's house stood on a level above Kōsaku's and looked as though it was firmly pressing it down. In fact, it was not just Kōsaku who was being pressed down and crushed—the whole community was being overwhelmed by the powerful Iwazō.

Some two years before, Kōsaku had gone to Yamanaka Hisajirō's place and asked for help getting a job for his younger brother Noboru. "It's my own younger brother. Can't you get help from someplace in Osaka? Couldn't you ask Ozaki for me?"

The request came from Yamanaka to Ozaki Sensei and from Sensei to my husband and me. Our suggestion was to apprentice the boy to an engraver, a man on thoroughly good terms with us, who had been go-between for our marriage and who through me had become obligated to Sensei. This man had been burned out in the great Kantō earthquake and fire of 1923, had come to Osaka from Tokyo, and had established himself as a tortoise-shell craftsman; he engraved decorations on tortoise-shell clasps, combs, hairpins and such. He was a skillful engraver, with much of the spirit of a master craftsman. But it was delicate fingertip work that strains the eyes and wears the nerves. Would it suit a boy fresh from the country?

Sensei asked the engraver, "If worst came to worst, even if Noboru's eyes lost their sight, would you be willing to take care of this youngster for the rest of your life?" It was characteristic that Sensei would do more than ask for a job for someone else, that he would consider the person's future and make the responsibility for it explicit. The engraver was an ordinary working man. "Yes, that's all right,"

Kotoe

he said firmly, "I'll look after him completely, just as though he were my own son." With that the matter should have been settled.

When Kōsaku brought Noboru to Osaka and went with Sensei to the engraver's home, I happened to be there. Noboru's suitcases were crammed tight with silk jackets, white shirts, *tabi* [split-toe stockings] and other clothes and accessories. All of them were brand new, with the price tags still on. Sensei teased him. "That's exactly the kind of baggage you make up for somebody going away as a bride or as an adopted husband, isn't it?" [An adopted husband is one who takes his wife's family name and inheritance. The practice is not unusual in Japan, and we will encounter several instances in these chapters. It occurs most often when a family has no sons and so "adopts" a man to marry a daughter, thus preserving the continuity of the family line. As a kind of "male bride," an adopted husband takes a "dowry" with him. A well-to-do family may establish separate households for its daughters, and adopt husbands for them rather than marry them into other families. Kōsaku, for example, took the Seki name when he married Iwazō's sister. It is another indication of the Seki family's wealth and power.]

Then Sensei said to Kōsaku, "Haven't you been grumbling all along like an old woman that this younger brother is more expensive than a clumsy, wasteful servant? Then take these high-priced things back with you and return them, tags and all, to the store where you bought them."

"What do you mean?" said Kōsaku, "We went to a lot of trouble to get these together." He was very reluctant, but finally he yielded. And he not only took back as it was all the luggage, he even had Noboru strip off the clothes he was wearing, including tabi and undershorts, and change into the clothes of a fellow apprentice who had been in the engraver's house for some time. When he saw the completely changed appearance of his younger brother, Kōsaku sobbed, "It's too much for me. Poor Noboru. Poor boy."

Sensei had said it would be best for young Noboru to live with the engraver in a spirit of having been picked up by the man and taken in naked, and that the engraver on his part must be responsible for the boy as though he were his own son; therefore neither of them should be concerned about any luggage or goods. When Kōsaku sighed for his younger brother, Sensei said at once, "There you are! For the first time in your life you've thought about your younger brother and cried! If I had sent you back to Kasama and let matters alone, without returning the luggage and the clothes he was wearing, you'd surely have taken the attitude that 'I have done everything an older brother can do.' Then as things went along, without meaning to, you'd forget all about your brother. Or even if you didn't, you would have gone all through life without ever tasting an elder brother's love for his younger brother the way you are now."

This had taken place in the middle of November, 1935. Then in January of 1936, when I visited Kasama for the first time, Kōsaku invited Sensei, Yamanaka and me to his house to thank us for helping find work for Noboru. Sensei and I said we had a previous engagement, that actually we had been invited to Iwazō's house; but Kōsaku urged us, "Well, anyway, come to my place first." We could hardly refuse, and when we stopped by, Kōsaku and his family treated us so hospitably it was as though they couldn't do enough for us. Outside, the air was so cold my skin hurt, but inside the room a charcoal stove was blazing, and warm vapor and a delicious savor were coming from the sukiyaki pan atop it. The members of the family came in one by one to repeat their thanks for our helping young Noboru and to urge us to dip into the pan.

At that point Iwazō entered. Since he and Kōsaku are brothers, he had no reason to feel constrained; but he thoughtlessly flopped down at ease, with a look as if to say that it was his own house. He struck an arrogant pose and paid no attention at all to the way Kōsaku, the head of the house, got up and down and diligently acted as a waiter. Iwazō brushed aside the members of the family with a glance. Picking up some meat with chopsticks, he started talking to Sensei.

"By the way, Ozaki, I . . . want to speak with you . . . . what I mean is . . ."

Whether he had a habit of saying things slowly or was doing it purposely, he spoke with pauses. To head off what was coming, Sensei said, "Yes, I understand. You don't have to say everything you are thinking of saying."

"Is that so? It's just like you." Iwazō seemed impressed. "Well, I, a few years ago . . . at Sakai, Osaka, had you buy me a cow, and the two of us led it back from Osaka together, didn't we? On the way back we talked about this—I mean you're a Tenri man and I'm a Christian, and I said Christ believed in giving up everything, and I can give up everything and live on. You said, 'Is that so? But what if there's something you just can't give up as a human being but should give up—it doesn't always fail to happen in a lifetime—what'll you do then?' So Ozaki, since you're my friend . . . doing something unconventional, smashing down an altar . . . your unconventional actions worry me. What I feel now is that I am in a situation where I cannot accept what I should accept. I want to discuss it and get a solution."

Iwazō looked dead serious. He did not seem drunk, nor to have come to pick a fight. But Sensei didn't act as though he very much wanted any part of it. "The source of these troubles of yours is not in something that just started suddenly. It's not like the recent earthquake: the epicenter is a long way off."

"Epicenter? Hah!" Iwazō's laugh was odd, a laugh that was about to be swallowed and then came out the nose. He was holding the chopsticks in his mouth.

Sensei said, "Laugh if you want, but that ache in your heart, in short what you cannot accept but must accept, is the matter of your family's financial situation."

"Right! You understand. Hah-hah!" Again that laugh of his; but I could readily tell that he really felt serious.

Iwazō's duties involved showing his face here and there every day, so it was no surprise that he neglected the farm tasks that were his family's occupation. The strain on the family budget came from that. On top of it all, his family was large and their upkeep costly. He had six younger brothers and sisters. Living nearby were the sister who had married Kōsaku, and a brother, Shinkichi, who had gone as an adopted husband to the Mihara house. (Shinkichi had been given some paddy as his adopted husband's "dowry.") In addition, two other brothers still were living at home and both were attending middle school. It is unusual for a farmer to be able to send sons and younger brothers to middle school. Furthermore, when yours is the most respected family in the village, you have to push yourself to maintain a prestige twice that of anyone else. So it was not just Sensei; anybody could easily imagine the pinch inside the Seki household regardless of its flourishing appearance.

Sensei parried. "There is an easy way to solve the problem. But even if I tell you, unless you're determined to carry it through, nothing will come of it no matter what I say. So it seems better for me not to say anything."

"Oh? Ozaki, please tell me."

"Are you sure you'll carry through?"

"If I don't hear what it is . . . there are things a man can carry through and things he can't. First I have to know what it is."

"If that's how you feel, I've decided not to say."

"Is it something easy or something hard?"

"Well, if you think of it as easy you will find nothing so easy, and if you think of it as hard you will really find it hard. Because it's a mental problem; I mean, it depends on how you feel about it."

Seki seemed to be thinking about how he could first get to hear Sensei's plans and then choose among them, while Sensei was thinking about the character of this friend who did not seem likely to carry matters through. But neither had the nerve to say what was on his mind, so the subtle jockeying continued, and the atmosphere gradually thickened.

"Come on, say it. Tell me about it."

"No, it seems better not to."

As these lines were repeated again and again, the fire in the stove dwindled and the food in the pan cooled. I wonder how long this verbal give-and-take might have continued? Sensei, with his natural disposition to be honest and not leave things done halfway, is not able to refuse directly when he is asked for advice; and once he has given it he feels responsible. Also, the other party was a difficult customer, not an easygoing type who would try to carry out somebody else's advice right away. It was not unreasonable for Sensei to be reluctant to speak.

As the atmosphere in the room grew more and more difficult to breathe, I began to worry about a heart attack. I just could not take any more, and though I realized it was impolite at a house you were visiting for the first time, I excused myself and went into the next room. It seemed to be a "lower room" with bedding spread out and heat in the *kotatsu* [covered brazier]. I slipped my hands and feet in and tried it, but they not only failed to warm up, they actually got chilly; and my head and face, and finally my hands and feet, began to quiver as though little insects were crawling all over them. My chest was heavy, and breathing hurt. Seeing my pale face, the surprised group all came over by my pillow. Since Sensei and Yamanaka knew about my attacks, they were not startled, but Seki Iwazō was badly shaken. He knelt by my pillow formally and said in a cracking voice, "I'm sorry that on my account you feel so bad."

I looked up and said, "It's a weakness I've always had. I'll be better soon, so please don't worry," and I closed my eyes.

Relieved, Seki got back his nerve and began again with Sensei. "If there is anything I can do to help myself, then I don't care what it is, I'll do it! I really will! So tell me."

Whether he saw that if he kept repeating himself the issue would not come to a head, or whether having seen me collapse he realized it was time now to put an end to the discussion, I don't know; but Seki's voice rang with decision. Even listening from the next room I could sense his concern. Perhaps he really was determined to go through with it. Sensei seemed to sense it too.

"If you'll promise that much, I'll tell you."

Even I could predict exactly what policy Sensei would offer. And not just me—anybody who lived in the village would know; it was something everybody knew and nobody would say. If you wonder why, it was because face to face with the powerful Seki Iwazō they didn't have the courage to say anything painful to his ears; or to put it another way, they were afraid of revenge from Seki, with his reputation for spreading malicious gossip. So nobody gave Seki straightforward advice. Sensei probably decided that if somebody had to brave slander and offer some sound advice, then as a close friend he should take the risk.

Sensei straightened his legs and sat formally, looked Seki in the face, and pushed his points forward one by one. "First, resign from all seven public offices. Then live by your land and concentrate everything on the family occupation. These offices are your father's 'seven glories'; aren't the villagers merely submitting to *that*? After all, it's not your own power. So you ought to give up all your positions and at one move become an ordinary man again; on that basis you can build a position on your own.

"Second, get younger brother Shinkichi to return the paddy he was given when he went as an adopted husband. That'll not only help the Seki family's finances, it'll do something more. I hear Shinkichi's parents-in-law are grumbling that 'adopt a husband from a good house and he's so cocky the family can't get along with him.' But if Shinkichi strips himself naked and tries to serve them humbly, maybe he can show them he's capable of effectively creating family harmony.

"Third, two younger brothers are going to middle school now but they should be made to withdraw right away. Since they've finished compulsory education, nobody will criticize if you get them good jobs somewhere, and it'll be a great relief to the family budget. Making two younger brothers quit school will ruin your face as elder brother—but isn't getting you into a more humble frame of mind what everybody in your family is secretly hoping for? If you did manage to get your brothers successfully graduated, then whenever the opportunity came up you'd think 'yes, it was thanks to me they did it.' And if they went out in the world and failed, you'd think 'oh, the rewards of virtue—after all the trouble I went to to send them to school,' and you wouldn't sympathize with them. That's why even if you hurt your reputation, making your younger brothers quit school now will give you a basis for future harmony between elder and younger brothers."

Giving his final blow, Sensei said "I haven't any right to force you, or any duty to. But because you insisted, I told you what I've always thought. If you think you really can't manage it, then believe in Christ and accept everything—I mean, accept the idea that it's all in the natural course of events. Because you happened to be born the eldest son of the Seki house, you're obligated to go on protecting the house and making it prosper. *I* think the Seki family property doesn't belong just to you alone. If there are seven brothers and sisters, there should be seven equal shares. But if you're not able to see it that way, then you haven't much choice but to do what I said."

At some point in Sensei's speech Seki stopped groaning and listened silently until it was over. Lying in the next room, I could picture his face clearly. No doubt it had a confused what-can-I-say expression, sulking, angry, cut to the quick.

When we left Kōsaku's house the day already had gone completely dark, and there were chilled-looking stars blinking in the night sky.

The next day Sensei met Shinkichi, told him part of the previous day's conversation, then said, "If you give the paddy back, you'll have to live more humbly in your adopted house, but that way the family will be contented. Because you'll hear your parents-in-law say 'It's much better that we got one from a poor family.' " Shinkichi thought about it for a while, then said, "That's really so; there's truth in it."

Since he hesitated—because even though he was willing to return the paddy, he had his adopted family to support at this point—Sensei said, "If that's the problem, the four families will buy the paddy from you and return it to Iwazō, and it'll be all right to pay us back whenever you're able to." Shinkichi seemed to breathe easier.

A day or two after this an unusually long letter from Seki Iwazō was delivered to Sensei's place. It was written by brush in an extremely good hand. But its contents amounted to an unmistakable declaration of war. Ignoring the fact that Seki himself had tenaciously begged Sensei to freely offer any advice he had, the letter said Sensei's suggestions were an overdone bit of mockery, an ill-meant slander that scarcely concealed foul feelings, and therefore Seki had disagreed with them from beginning to end. Then came the following words:

"Which of us is superior, you or I? Let us test our strength."

The challenge did not end with words, it soon showed up in deeds. Here young Noboru's affairs again became an issue.

Soon after the declaration of war Iwazō went to Kōsaku's place and vented his anger and distrust. "Ozaki hasn't got any business being that helpful to other people. No doubt it's some sort of scheme. If we dally, there's no telling what a bad time we'll have." Raging on, he strongly urged that younger brother Noboru be brought back at once. You can't contradict what is said half in command by the fearsome face of a powerful elder brother-in-law of a main house. What Kōsaku himself was thinking deep in his heart I don't know, but without giving the engraver any explanation he hurriedly brought home Noboru who was just managing to settle into his new occupation.

Dragged back without a chance to say how he felt about it, Noboru soon was sent as adopted husband to a family related to the Yamanakas. This was unquestionably

42

a tactical marriage. That is, Yamanaka's relatives gained control of an official hamlet position as compensation for taking Noboru. Furthermore, the position was one that previously had been filled by Sensei's elder brother Ritarō. Seki Iwazō had power enough to force through a senseless action like that.

There is no doubt that Ritarō and Yamanaka both felt betrayed. And it was especially true of Sensei. Gentle and patient as he is, even Sensei was furious about this treatment. "I can see that if Noboru is still with his adopted family three years from now, I won't be alive in this world any more." [That is, Ozaki would get revenge on Seki for his actions, or die trying.] Since he let slip things like that, you know he was thoroughly enraged. However, possibly it was coincidence but before three years had passed, Noboru got pains in his chest and died a lonely death while trying to recuperate in a rented room in a temple. In any case, bringing Noboru back was the first step in Seki's determined plot to do Ozaki in.

Misunderstanding breeds new misunderstanding. Soon after Noboru was brought back Iwazō warned Shinkichi that it wouldn't do to be around Ozaki, that he seemed to have some kind of plot on his mind. Shinkichi, who had accepted Sensei's proposal, broke off his agreement to give the paddy back. It was bad enough to see Sensei's good intentions come to naught, but it meant that by doing this Shinkichi himself ruined the opportunity he had purposely set up for solving his difficulties with his adopted family.

Iwazō's detestable hand then reached out to the Tenri Chapel. He went to the Chief's house and threatened him, "Smashing an altar is against the criminal code, so don't listen to what Ozaki says; build a new altar. If you don't there'll be much trouble." The Chief hadn't been able to agree deep in his heart with nephew Ozaki, and he was on the verge of secretly being sorry he had acted on the spur of the moment. Moreover, he was so deeply involved with Seki for his livelihood that when he heard Seki's threat he immediately went limp. At once he notified Sensei and the four families that the altar was to be rebuilt and asked if they would please agree to it. The four families replied that if that happened they would stop supporting the chapel.

However, this move—which had been so marvelously effective before—didn't seem to work this time. They expected him to cringe, but the Chief said in full confidence, "All right. Even if you four families quit, Seki said the whole village will support me so I'm not afraid. I want the four families to leave the Church."

This was why less than a month after it had been smashed the altar in the chapel was rebuilt. Of course, a great consecration ceremony was held with Seki Iwazō as leader. And during February, March and April the village faithful came one after another just as before to bow to the altar and go home again. The whole affair had been like a mountain laboring to give birth to a mouse. But it would still have been good if it had ended there.

I suppose it was in the latter third of April that Sensei and I were walking over the Nagaizaka slope. It's about two kilometers from Kasama to Hase, which is famous for its tree-peonies, and to get there you have to cross Nagaizaka. You go to the top of Chōja Yashiki, and then down a rock-strewn steep road. We changed to straw sandals, and wrapped our clogs in a *furōshiki* [carrying cloth]. Although it was the flower season and still a little chilly in the day-time, as we walked the steep slope our sweat came off in big drops. Suddenly we saw the face of the Chapel Chief. He seemed a little surprised to see us too, and when Sensei asked, "Chief, where are you going?," he said, "Oh, well, just over to Hase Police Box. Well, excuse me," and went off down Nagaizaka at a ridiculously fast pace. If we had been more sensitive we might have had a premonition of what was going to happen from his strangely flustered behavior; but at the time we did not pay much attention to it.

Only ten days after this, at the end of April, there was a call from the Hase Police Box for Sensei and me. It was a summons for four of us—Sensei, Yamanaka, Mitani, and myself. Being summoned by the police was not anything to take calmly. The four of us tried to figure out what in the world was wrong, but we could not think of anything other than the altar-smashing affair. We decided that if *that* was the matter, it would not be serious; they would understand once we explained it to them.

The Sergeant looked at us and said abruptly, "Did you call at Seki's place?" [before reporting to the Station]. We caught on then for the first time that Seki apparently had been the one who had complained to the police. We had been pretty naive. We simply had not expected anybody to file a complaint, and would not have dreamed it of Seki. Then when we saw the Chapel Chief, who must have come to the police box before we did, sitting stiffly before the Sergeant and not even turning his face in our direction, we finally caught on to his odd behavior at Nagaizaka. Seki had challenged Sensei to a test of strength but to exert his power he had to borrow the arm of the law.

The Sergeant became aggressive. "The matter of smashing an altar is a crime of irreverence. What method did you use in destroying the gods?"

The Chief, cowering in fear, answered in a trembling voice, "Well, . . . I put on a mask, and after washing my hands I set aside the sacred objects." Actually the Chief was the one who had directly handled them. If we were to be punished for what we had instigated, he certainly would not escape scot-free.

Next I spoke in some detail, from my own point of view, about what Sensei said at Seki's house, and about Sensei's state of mind as a missionary. And Sensei explained point by point, without shrinking back, the matters we were

45

being questioned about. Since the Seki-Ozaki discord (or more precisely Seki's one-sided hatred) was a local affair, the Sergeant had naturally gotten wind of it. I wonder if he had already made up his mind who was to blame? But anyway since Seki was the most powerful man in the village the Sergeant couldn't completely ignore his complaint. Was that why he had started off by badgering us about crimes of irreverence?

The Sergeant thought about our words for a while in silence, then lifted his head and said, "In short, it's nothing but a personal conflict between Mr. Ozaki and Mr. Seki, isn't it? Well, that's not a police matter. Since it's a messy local affair, see if you can work it out calmly, will you?"

In other words, once he heard our side too, the situation was all right. We had thought so, of course, but to be honest we were relieved. The Sergeant caught hold of the Chief as he was about to leave and slapped him firmly on the back, "Buck up, old man!" We were well aware that he was criticizing the Chief by teasing him, and it probably echoed in the Chief's ears.

What a delight to have the pressure that had been weighing on us for several days suddenly disappear. It seemed a little early in the season yet for the tree-peonies of Nagaya temple, but here and there already the lamp-like peonies were beautiful. We walked through the flowers. Though I'm apt to get a little melancholy in places like this, I felt a sense of revival to have discovered that outside the village there were understanding people like the Sergeant. Even though it was pointless to get mad about Iwazō's foul actions, still he was a vile man. Perhaps in a situation of this sort you can say he was returning evil for good. At any rate this day was a day to remember for several reasons, so I said we should have a picture taken; and the five of us— Sensei, Yamanaka, Imanishi, Mitani and I—had a souvenir photo taken of ourselves amid the peonies.

46

Three months passed. We had forgotten all about the incident. And since as far as we knew the police had accepted what we said and had agreed with us, the case should have been closed. But in fact it was not. We had forgotten, but the police and Seki had not forgotten for a minute.

Because the well at Sensei's family's place needed relocating, Sensei and I came back from Osaka as usual to lend a hand. Yamanaka would drop everything and hurry over whenever he'd hear Sensei was back, so naturally he was there early in the morning to help; so were Imanishi and Mitani. We managed to finish the job by evening, thanks to everybody pooling their efforts; we were relaxing and sipping tea when an unfamiliar middle-aged man in a business suit came in. He was in charge of the Special High Police detachment at the Sakurai station. [The Special High Police were entrusted with thought-control.]

"Mr. Ozaki, I want you to come along with me to the Sakurai station. And I want that woman to come, too."

His attitude was peremptory. We wondered what was up—it was already evening—but since we knew perfectly well that if we tried to refuse they would make it hard on us later, Sensei and I began to get ready to leave. At that moment Sensei's four-year-old son Shunji for some reason suddenly burst out crying as though he'd been burned. He did not have enough understanding yet to know his father was being led away, but perhaps because he sensed the tense atmosphere he wouldn't stop. The Special High Police Chief relented.

"Tomorrow morning's okay. I'd like you to be there by nine."

Sensei's mother was in a flurry, moving about nervously, asking "What is it?" I tried to console her, "When he heard the boy crying, he said tomorrow morning is good enough and left, so it can't be anything serious." I didn't have a glimmering of what it might be. Whatever they might accuse me of, my conscience said I had nothing of which to be ashamed. Still I was discouraged to think that I had been summoned by the police again and would have to explain things in detail once more.

The next morning Sensei and I went to the station. Chief Yoshimura of the Special High Police said to come by nine. When we stopped a policeman and told him this, he said he would check on it and went inside but didn't come back. Nine o'clock passed, then nine-thirty. By ten o'clock we still had not heard a word. The policemen we spoke to only stared at us; they didn't say "come this way" or "go home," they just left us there. The two of us sat waiting on a bench just to the right of the station door. There was nothing we *could* do but wait. Finally, when it was close to eleven, we were sent into the room marked "Special High." Sitting in his chair, Chief Yoshimura, a man a bit past forty, glanced at us and pointed our way to chairs by thrusting out his chin.

At last the questioning began. Yoshimura turned to Sensei, "Now then, you seem to be trying to spread a new religion, so I'd like you to tell me a little about its doctrines."

"Doctrines? There aren't any."

"But you've quit Tenri."

"No, I haven't quit Tenri at all."

"If that's so, why did you destroy the gods?"

"Destroy the gods? That's wrong. I destroyed an altar."

"Ah ha! Gods or altar, it's the same thing. You destroyed the gods and left Tenri."

"No, Tenri left me."

"What's that supposed to mean? You left Tenri because you destroyed the gods. That's why I said you must have some other religion. What a fool!"

"No, I don't have any."

"But if you left Tenri, you've got to have another religion. Let's hear its doctrines." Gradually the Chief became peevish. His voice grew rough. "Hm? Tell me—its doctrines!" He began shouting. But Sensei still was silent, not saying a word, perhaps because he thought it would not do any good even if he tried to explain, or perhaps because he thought there was nothing he needed to explain.

Chief Yoshimura played his trump. "What am I going to do with you two? In order to cool off you need to take a purifying bath and think a while. How about it, do you want to stay overnight at the station?"

Sensei will fight to the finish against attempts to high-handedly force anything unjust. But because he tends to interpret things very simply, when the Chief said we should stay at the station, take a purifying bath and think things over for a while, Sensei showed signs of simply agreeing that perhaps we ought to do so.

When I saw what was happening, I thought: this is ridiculous, we aren't going to be kept over night by a trick like this; and I guessed that it was another of Seki's schemes. I said to the Chief, "I have a request. I'd like you to listen to our views for a minute."

Suddenly he smiled, "M-hm. Tell me. Let's hear your views." He apparently misunderstood and thought that by 'views' [shinkyō] I meant some new doctrine [shinkyō] we took after leaving Tenri.

"Chief, what I mean by 'views' isn't some new teaching but our state of mind." With that introduction I told him all about what had happened, from my own motives for joining Tenri to Sensei's decision to smash the altar and leave mission work because of his child's misfortune; then about how Seki had asked for advice because his family had him worried, and how for that reason he and Sensei had had a sudden falling-out. The Chief listened quietly and said nothing. When my explanation was done, a uniformed policeman coughed and rushed into the room, pulled out two postcards from his pocket and laid them before the Chief. Then he turned to Sensei and drew himself up gravely as though he was about to say something, but the Chief stopped him, "All right, all right, that's enough. Thanks. Go out there."

The two postcards the Chief now handed over to Sensei were ones Sensei had sent to his home, and at the end of the message in both cases they mentioned his mother. When the Chief had asked Sensei earlier, "What are you thinking about most of all right now?", Sensei had answered, "Most of all I'm worried about my mother." Since the postcards backed it up, the Chief didn't have any way to disprove it. He tried to see if he could pressure Sensei with some shrewd questions, but thanks to Sensei's way of not being cowardly or playing tricks or double-dealing, it was wasted effort. As a result, the charge of starting an unauthorized religion evaporated, and we were able to return home the same day. In fact the Chief even said, "That really took up a lot of time; shall we get some lunch?" But Sensei said, "We have to get back because my mother will be worrying."

As we walked along the road across the pass, the villagers we met poured stares of curiosity on us but kept their mouths shut. At the Ozaki house Yamanaka, Imanishi and Mitani were anxiously waiting for us. Yamanaka said, "Kakutani's been saying there's a rumor around the village that Ozaki and the four families are really in for it now." Kakutani was a relative of Yamanaka's, and seemed to think it best for Yamanaka to break off with Ozaki as soon as he could. The whole village was full of talk about Sensei's visit to the station.

"Anybody who gets hauled into the station must be a bad one."

"The way it looks now, he's really in a fix."

We didn't even need to ask whether this backbiting resulted from string-pulling by Seki Iwazō.

There was an obvious reason why the two of us had been made to wait so long at the station. That is, the uniformed policeman who had rushed into the Special High office with the postcards had made use of that time to search the Ozaki house. From what Sensei's mother said, the policeman (whose name was Shimazaki) flaunted the power of his office and came right up onto the mats with his shoes on, yelled "Which is Ozaki's bedroom?," charged through the rooms and threw everything into disorder. When he realized that there was nothing of use to him, he said, "There must be letters Ozaki sent from Osaka," and he took away two postcards from among the mail Sensei's mother showed him. Ordinarily she was a sturdy woman, but this time she was crying. "I'm so ashamed that all the neighbors were watching, I can't bear it."

CHAPTER FIVE
Abandoning a corpse

Our tangles with the police were not done yet. The issue that came next was over Imanishi Kunimatsu's funeral. Although in one sense the result was "misery turned to blessing," for a while it looked as if we'd be charged with abandoning a corpse, and all of us involved were kept in suspense.

Imanishi Kunimatsu wrote the following will on December 5, 1936 and died on the 25th.

WILL

Because of illness I had been a believer in Tenri for many years, had listened to its teachings, had contributed funerary implements and many days of service as well. But it was merely a formality and I performed it without any benefit. Realizing since early this year that my attitude had changed, I came to accept the faith that passes directly from father to son, elder brother to younger brother, and on to all kinsmen. Truly in this world there is nothing a parent loves so much as his child, and I am satisfied that there is no doctrine greater than pure-hearted filial piety between parents and children. So after I die I will not listen to any funeral orations or eulogies; I need no formal Buddhist or Shintō ceremonies; I will be satisfied just to be wrapped in a coarse straw mat and buried by the hands of the group. I ask this of Tokuichi.

Kunimatsu
December 5, 1936

It was the last thing written by Kunimatsu, whose kidneys had gone bad that summer. He wrote it carefully, letter by letter, using his brush as he lay in bed, having his wife Yasue hold the paper. And though I would criticize some parts of it, the gist of it was that after he died no formal funeral would be necessary.

For forty long years this man had earnestly believed in Tenri, given up the tobacco he enjoyed, and taken his money and goods to the church while his family lived a cramped life. Whenever there was a funeral among the faithful, he took part in the ceremonies, performing the duties a priest handles for Buddhists. He also went whenever labor was being donated without pay, since it would accumulate hidden blessings. Looked at superficially Kunimatsu was a true believer of a rare sort. But if you ask whether his feelings were completely satisfied by the faith, you can't deny that there's room for doubt. In particular, as a grandfather he was especially worried whenever he thought about his granddaughter's condition.

While she still was a baby, the family talked about how her ankles looked too straight; but they didn't do anything about it and left her that way, and by the time she was three or four she had become a hopeless cripple. Maybe the family had been careless, but they probably didn't do anything because they were caught in the framework of Tenri belief.

Tenri insists that "The feet are tools for carrying. If those carrying tools are diseased, it is proof that you are carrying inadequately. So if you do not carry to the church at once, your bad karma ties will not be broken." The deeply faithful Imanishi family took those feet to church of course, and also carried all the money and goods they could. Soon the granddaughter turned five. Since she couldn't wear ordinary clogs, she always wore boots and walked on her instep. Her soles were turned outward. The family carried to that church as if their lives depended on it, but the shape of her feet didn't seem to change one bit. At first the family seems to have hidden it even from relatives like the Ozakis, but once Sensei heard of it, he said, "What a stupid thing to be doing," and urged them to take her to an Osaka hospital at once.

Taking the Imanishi father and daughter along with him to his house in Osaka, Sensei walked the streets daily in search of a doctor. There were any number of corrective surgeons, but the Imanishis couldn't afford an expensive operation. At the surgical section of the Sumida Hospital, when he was shown photographs of marvellously corrected conditions, father Tokuichi couldn't wait any more and appealed to Sensei, "Even if I have to sell my house and fields, if I have to become a beggar, I don't care so long as I get her feet as straight as these."

But Sensei had worries of his own. Not only was he being bitterly denounced by the church, but he didn't have any way to pay the surgical fees. Tokuichi hadn't had time to think about what would happen afterward; he was only thinking about getting the child's feet to look like other people's. But what would happen to the eight people in his family when the operation was over and they realized that they were financially stripped? They already had given everything to the church and had nothing to spare. Something had to be done for the future of the house. In any case, you couldn't expect Sensei to have a cent of savings from the kind of monkish life he was leading as a missionary.

"I feel responsible. I'll do whatever has to be done to find a sympathetic doctor for you."

Repeating this to himself, Sensei walked the streets day after day. Picture a father carrying his daughter on his back, the lower half of her body wrapped in a blanket, her cheek resting on his shaved head, followed by a Tenri missionary in cotton kimono and *hakama* [formal skirt worn over a kimono]; the father was thinking only of his love for his child, the missionary overflowed with sincerity and truth —two hearts and three shapes in search of a doctor. Finally

Sensei committed professional suicide. Knocking at the gate of a doctor's place, he asked, in all honesty, "Inasmuch as these people have given all their wealth to the Tenri Church and still are in agony about their girl's feet, can't you help us out?"

The doctor listened silently, then said, "I understand. Thank you for coming, but I'm not a corrective surgeon; my sign says surgeon but I'm an internal surgeon. So there's nothing I can do for you." However, when he saw how discouraged Sensei and Tokuichi were, he was moved to sympathize. After a moment he seemed to make up his mind and said, "Well then, let's ask one of my younger colleagues. You see, he's just opened his practice, and if he wants the experience, he may do it for nothing if we ask him to." He wrote a note of introduction and soon contacted the man by phone.

The other doctor quickly came to meet them. It was like "being in hell and meeting the Buddha." Things progressed by leaps and bounds, and they spent several days busy with her hospitalization and the operation. During that time Sensei and Tokuichi both were completely caught up in the matter. Finally the day came to take off the cast. Under the watchful eyes of a father unable to hold back his anxiety, the doctor deftly began to remove the cast but after a time said "uuh" in a low voice. And then, "Oh! It's a little short."

He didn't mean the operation had failed, of course. But because the knitted bones were a little short, the soles of her feet were not quite back where they should be. "If we do it over again, she'll recover completely," the doctor said with great regret, but father Tokuichi didn't have the courage to listen to the sound of the surgical axe a second time and he declined another operation. Even if it was just a little short or long, if the soles of her feet managed to face down and she was at least able to wear clogs, that was good enough. At any rate, now she was freed from the sorrow of being considered a cripple. She could have hopes for life. With tears in their eyes, Tokuichi and Sensei thanked this wonderful doctor again and again, and they went home with their faces transformed by joy.

When grandfather Kunimatsu saw the figure of his beloved granddaughter now, he got the nerve to strike out on his own for the first time. By then he had lost his good will towards Tenri, and of course he was influenced by the fact that soon afterward Sensei smashed the altar and explained to him why it had to be done.

When Kunimatsu died, nobody from the Tenri Church would come to conduct a funeral, since the Imanishis had followed Sensei and done away with their home altar. Nor did the family see any need to hold Buddhist services; so all they could do was follow Kunimatsu's will. The will said, "by the hands of the group." This referred to the four families, so Sensei and the four families gathered around Tokuichi to discuss the problem. During vigil-night the relatives argued bitterly over whether or not to hold an informal funeral, and the most effective argument was that if we did anything that silly we'd be sure to regret it. However, Tokuichi as chief mourner honored his late father's wishes to the letter, and said decisively that it would be done as the will ordered.

The day of the funeral arrived. Many people came from the neighborhood and from nearby villages. By rural custom, a funeral is a kind of village-wide celebration, except for blood relatives directly linked to the deceased—"the old man's funeral is the grandchildren's festival." It is one day when the crew of neighborhood wives bustling about in the kitchen can eat to their heart's content. The husbands, free of work clothes and dressed in the formal kimono they wear only a few times a year, go out in threes and fives to invite people to come. It's ridiculous to talk about "simplification of ceremonies." If that happened, one of our life's pleasures would be taken away. You can't easily throw away an unexpected opportunity to eat and drink for two or three days in a row. This time too, as usual, crowds of people were coming and going constantly.

The will said "wrapped in a coarse straw mat," but since we couldn't bring ourselves to do that under any circumstances, we just put him in a coffin. And since the coffin alone was too crude—it seemed impolite to the soul of the deceased—we wrapped a foot-wide strip of bleached cotton around and around it.

Finally the ceremony began: a funeral like none ever heard of before. A grave-marker made from a smoothly planed board was set up in front of the coffin, which had been put in an inner room. Chief mourner Tokuichi slowly took up the marker and wrote on it in black ink "Grave of Imanishi Kunimatsu," turned it over and added on the back "Died December 25, 1936." Then he bowed his head politely time after time. One after another the members of the four families did the same. Not a word was said during all this. It wasn't very dramatic, but when the solemn respects had been paid, Tokuichi said quietly, "Now the relatives, please feel free to offer your respects as you feel them in your heart."

The relatives all came forward by turns and paid their respects the same way. The only thing different was that they had Buddhist rosaries in their hands.

Without our noticing it a crowd of people had pressed in under the eaves outside the room and were gawking at the sight of this odd funeral. Ordinarily the "guests" have a good time drinking and eating, but this time they seemed to forget the food and liquor; they were breathing quietly, maybe because they were moved by curiosity about the kind of funeral that would be held by this group who had destroyed the Tenri gods.

By and by, when all the relatives had paid their respects, a command suddenly issued from among the standees, "All together! Bow!" People didn't even have time to think about it; at once they mechanically obeyed the command and gave the deepest of bows. "They made fools of us," people grumbled afterward, "That's the first time I've gone to a funeral and been made to bow." But in the atmosphere of the moment it seemed completely natural to me.

The burial procession consisted of the neighborhood pallbearers, Tokuichi carrying the grave marker, the four families, and the relatives, in that order. When the grave had been dug and the coffin was about to be lowered in, I said without thinking, "Wait a minute! It's a shame to bury that cloth on the coffin; let me take it," and I stripped it off. I suppose it was a queer thing to do. Some people may have thought it cruel. I don't care for things that have been close to the skin of a dead person; but I wasn't considering the feelings of the spectators, I was just thinking how wasteful it would be to bury that cloth.

Since they had carried out an unprecedented funeral, Sensei and the four families were emotionally exhausted. Even so, they were relieved that it had gone off without a hitch. Other people were not, however. Apparently there were many rumors. And at last another summons came from the police. Once again Seki Iwazō had informed on us. The police seemed to want to punish us for the crime of abandoning a corpse, but since I'd brought along Kunimatsu's will, there wasn't much that needed explaining. Chief Yoshimura said, "If the will called for it, you couldn't do much else," and that's how it ended.

The reason why the relatives were carrying Buddhist rosaries was this. The village has a Zen temple called Yōanji. As soon as they heard that Ozaki Sensei had smashed the Kasama altar, all the Tenri people in the village (except the four families) became supporters of the temple. The priest of the temple at first was baffled but delighted that the number of his supporters had increased so suddenly, but as the days passed the new members proved to be not such a blessing; and when he was over at our place, he spoke indignantly about "stingy good-for-nothing supporters!" He had guessed what was on their minds. [Since the Chapel Chief had taken part in the altar-smashing, he could not conduct funerals and prayers. So the villagers affiliated nominally with the Buddhist temple, in order to be able to call upon the priest to conduct these services. But they were not serious Buddhists, and they paid him only token fees.]

This meat-eating, sake-drinking priest was a favorite of ours. Sensei was sorry about the lukewarm supporters and was generous to the man. One time he said to the priest, "I'd like you to comfort the souls of the dead," asked him to chant a sutra, and gave him much more than the usual fee. It was Sensei's way of being kind. As the chanting began, Sensei said, "Priest, do you think the dead hear the sutra?" which made everybody laugh.

"Uh. Well, I don't know."

"If the lines in the sutra are difficult even for the living, won't they be all the more so for the dead? Let's let it go at that."

"I guess so. We'll let it go," said a pleased priest—pleased at not having to chant the whole long sutra.

Kunimatsu's funeral had a great influence on us later. I mean that our Shinkyō funerals have by and large been patterned on his, and eventually they became standardized in this informal form. A human being is capable of receiving treatment while he's ill; but when he becomes a corpse, let a day and a night pass and he's just a pile of filth giving off a horrible stench. You don't have to have ostentatious ceremonies in order to dispose of a corpse in a cemetery. Do your work until sundown, and when you're through it'll be enough if you simply divide the funeral tasks among those who'll dig the grave, those who'll put the corpse into the coffin, those who'll carry it to the cemetery, and so on. The form you choose is up to the deceased and those connected with him.

We neither reject religion nor by any means intend to be disrespectful to the deceased. It's simply that we believe that religion should never become a funeral tool or take on the role of a substitute doctor.

Several years after this we moved to Manchuria, as I'll tell about later. There in the year after the war ended (in August, 1945), eight of our group died from malnutrition. All our clothes were stolen by the Manchurians so we hadn't any to spare for the dead, and we couldn't do anything but bury them naked in the district schoolyard. We had our hands full just staying alive, and the last thing we had time to think about was a proper funeral. The number of grave-mounds in the schoolyard increased daily. The police ordered us to bury them in the public cemetery, but since we didn't have money for it, we tricked the watchman and just levelled off the mounds in the schoolyard. The bodies of those who died on the way back were buried at sea. There was a Buddhist priest with us in Manchuria, and since he had created posthumous names for the eight who died [a common practice in Japanese Buddhism], one of the survivors recorded them on a scrap of paper. And when the survivors rejoined those of us who still were in Japan, we burned the paper in a brazier and said, "The dead have also returned and are pleased to be on their home ground. Now for the first time they have gone to Heaven." That was our funeral. And I think it was a good one.

However, we do dream of building a cemetery in the future. It won't be a gloomy graveyard where ghosts seem about to dash out, but cheerful like a playground—it'll be on a hillside with cherry trees blooming all around on both sides of the road leading to it, and old folk and youngsters will picnic under the trees. In the center we'll have seesaws, swings, and slides; and the children will be playing with happy voices. On the south side there'll be a pond for boat-

ing. And the flowers of each of the four seasons will completely cover the great stone tablet marked "Shinkyō
Members." We'll think of our ancestors as being asleep in
this tomb, and about how some day we'll sleep there too.

CHAPTER SIX

Ostracism

The ties between Ozaki Sensei and the four families grew firm as they struggled through many trials and hardships. But the other side—the village power clique led by Seki Iwazō—reacted to this with an ever more obvious plan to drive Sensei out. And I think the rivalry between the two sides had reached the point where there had to be a clear settlement soon or there would be no peace.

On August 10, 1937, the Seki faction assembled the people of the eastern section of Kasama in the Tenri Chapel, which also was used as a hamlet meeting hall, and summoned Sensei there. He knew perfectly well what they had in mind, but since he saw no need to hide, he went to the meeting cool and composed. As they had planned, one after another of the Seki faction roundly denounced him.

"You're a troublemaker who's disturbing the peace of the village."

"Have you managed to do anything but disrespectful work like burning the gods?"

"Didn't you cheat an old man and hold a funeral that as much as threw away the corpse?"

"If these things are going to keep on and on, we've got to consider what'll happen to the village. What in hell are you thinking of?"

In short they closed in on him, counted up and reviewed his "crimes" to date. They probably calculated that once he was faced by the power of the majority even the obstinate Ozaki would humble himself. But Sensei wasn't bothered a bit. "If you mean the altar affair or that about Kunimatsu's burial," he said, "those didn't come from any arbitrary decision on my part. Far from it: weren't they done only after everybody had talked them over and agreed to them? So what the hell is wrong? You talk about disrupting the village, but aren't those who go crying to the cops and secretly pulling strings the real disturbers of the 'peace of the village'? They're right here among us. Do you want me to name names, or let it go at that?"

As Sensei spoke out so sharply and glared around, the gabbling assembly fell silent. Everybody had a guilty conscience. They hadn't foreseen that "poke in the brush and the snakes come out"; they were completely flustered and didn't say another word.

Sensei said, "Well then, it's better that I hold off naming names for this meeting. After this I'm going to refuse any calls on petty problems. I have nothing more to say, so it's best for you all to discuss it by yourselves." He hurried out, and not a single man tried to stop him.

Later I heard that, lost for a place to take out their anger, the Seki gang eventually concentrated their attack on the Chapel Chief, accusing him of being negligent. Then to make it worse they tore up the chapel before they left.

That gang was as persistent as could be. On the next day, the 11th, a summons came for Yamanaka and Mitani. First the gang surrounded Yamanaka and made him sit alone in the center.

"Break off with Ozaki!"

"If a good farmer like you tags along with a dangerous drifter like Ozaki," they said, "what do you think's going to happen in the future? We don't say you've done wrong, but break off with Ozaki today at this meeting and we'll see that you get a voice in village affairs." Such was their carrot-and-stick strategy. Knowing what had happened the day before with Ozaki Sensei, Yamanaka perceived the danger in the situation and was, as he put it, "scared silly." If he refused their demands here, what would come next? Considering how they operated, he could expect the worst. The tangled power relationships in the village were clear to him. And he was fully aware that there was no reason that he couldn't find a way to compromise or make excuses. But as Yamanaka himself told me later, "Before I thought about being hurt or helped or anything else, I lost my temper at Seki and the rest of that gang, with their stinking proud attitude and their trying to force things their way; and I couldn't help what I did."

Yamanaka lifted his face and said to them, "He hasn't done a thing wrong. What he says is right. I won't leave him even if it kills me."

Afterward he told me, "I was so afraid that my body was quivering, but I said what I had to say."

Next Mitani was called in and given exactly the same grilling. But Mitani also refused then and there, and said firmly that he would go along with Ozaki.

What Seki and his gang had reckoned was that Yamanaka and Mitani, who actually were living in the village and caught up in its many ties, surely would be won over. Once *they* turned against Ozaki, anything could be done to him if he was without local support. But the scheme fell apart at every step. The Seki faction had lost face.

"We can't put up with people who've got the mad idea that they'll stick together to the death"—this was their reason for village ostracism. Of course we didn't have any way of knowing when and how it was decided; and there was no formal announcement. We didn't learn of it for some weeks. Nobody, not even a relative, was permitted to speak to any member of the four families; and a stiff rule was made that anybody who spoke even once would be fined one hundred yen [equal to $100 at that time].

The members of the four families were treated as if they didn't exist. They were stripped of all human rights. City people can't even imagine what a painful position you're driven into when you suffer village ostracism. They know that in the old days there were tragedies aplenty because of village ostracism, but here even within their own lifetimes this vile tradition still was in full operation. Hemmed in by the ostracism, the four families had to resort to any means they could find in order just to keep alive during the war. [The war with China had begun July 7, 1937.]

The influence of the China War gradually reached out even to this little mountain village. Recruits began to leave in ones and twos.

By village custom, when a recruit was to be seen off, the first thing would be for the "walker," the village errand-boy, to go around the day before and call at each house announcing that "Tomorrow K—— of the S—— family leaves for the army, so come and say farewell." But even the walker avoided the four families. As the proverb says, "Gods you avoid won't hurt you." Since they could be fined even for opening their mouths, nothing at all was communicated to the four families officially.

Even so they waited expectantly, doubting that the silent treatment would continue in this situation. After all, saying farewell to a recruit was held to be a citizen's duty; neglecting it would be the same as treason—or so they thought. But not a word came. Eventually unable to stand it, they slipped out unseen and came to discuss the situation with Sensei in his house in Osaka. Sensei warned them seriously, "We may hate them as imperfect human beings for trampling on our duties as citizens. But since there's no question that we are Japanese citizens, out of respect for the red sash the right thing to do is to see off the recruit. So go ahead and join the farewell party."

Advised and encouraged this way, they came back to Kasama early the next morning acting as though nothing had happened.

At a signal from firecrackers, the recruit, his family and

kin, and the villagers all assembled in the grounds of the hamlet guardian shrine. There, after a prayer for good fortune, the recruit would give a formal farewell and set out, seen off by the headman, the militia, the women's club, and others. But the people passed coldly by the four families; nobody said a word.

The shrine grounds buzzed with the sound of voices, and everybody was rushing up and down the stone stairs at the entry. The recruit in his red sash climbed the stairs. The team from the women's club, the youth group—they all merely glanced at the four families and moved on. As you start up the stairs there is a stone dog on either side. And what you saw hiding in the shadows of the dogs—those pitiful human figures—were the members of the four families.

Then Teijirō, a relative of the recruit, came up. When they saw him, the members of the four families timidly moved out from behind the dogs and called to him to stop.

"This . . . it's a going-away present for the soldier. Couldn't you hand it to him for us?"

With a sour face Teijirō said, "We can't accept anything like this from people who've been ousted from the village."

What an insult! So furious they couldn't even cry, the four families ground their teeth in indignation. But faithful to Sensei's request to put up with it for the sake of the red sash, they turned and found a man who was related to the recruit but who, because he lived far away, hadn't heard about the ostracism, and they asked him to deliver the present.

The farewell party went as far as Sakurai. Because it was summer, when they reached Sakurai a watermelon was given to every person in the party. But the four families got none. A small rising-sun flag also was given to everyone, but not a one to the four families. It's ridiculous for dis-

Kotoe

crimination to be so literal, but at the time they weren't laughing: they needed all their strength to choke back tears of mortification.

These scenes were repeated eight times in all—eight different times that recruits left. Not that recruiting stopped after the eighth time, but we couldn't take any more after that. We very plainly saw a likelihood that we would be slandered as traitors or as un-Japanese because we didn't participate, but even Sensei had by then stopped talking about respect for the red sash. So instead of appearing at patriotic farewells, the four families eagerly threw their energies into farm work. "A farmer fulfills his duties by working hard on his farm," Sensei told them, "He risks his life in a farmer's way—by fighting the soil."

So they didn't take part in women's club meetings, bamboo-spear drills, and the like. They knew that if they tried to take part, the others would reject them. Thus the Seki faction had made outcasts of us and at the same time had humiliated us as "non-conformist traitors to national policy." The challenge that Seki Iwazō had flung at Sensei had begun to pay off.

The Eve—in Kasama this is the greatest event of the whole year, and a day for rest and relaxation.

Almost two months had passed in ostracism by the first of November, 1937, when the Eve came around. By then all contact between the four families and the villagers had been completely cut off, starting with the farewell parties and extending to weddings, death-day anniversaries, and all other celebrations.

The day before the Eve, Sensei and I came back from Osaka. As we went through the village from west to east to get to Sensei's home, somehow things around us looked odd. In the western section, where every house was bubbling with the excitement of preparing for the Eve by pounding ricecakes and so on, the Imanishi house was silent. Had they fled to the Ozaki place? As we passed through the central section and into the eastern one we could hear singing coming from the blacksmith's house with great shouting voices. It appeared to start all of a sudden when they caught sight of Sensei and me. They had carried a mortar out in front of the house and were pounding ricecakes there, but when I asked Sensei about it he said people ordinarily didn't do it that way. So we could only take it as an ill-meant bit of showing off.

That day at Sensei's home we pounded ricecakes and prepared a feast just like anybody else. And the following day all the members of the four families, old and young, male and female, carried the feast and the ricecakes and fled to Hirao Saime. Hirao Saime is the boundary between Kasama and a place in Uda county called Hirao. The Yamanakas have a field there. In that field the four families held their festival and "relaxation."

As we had decided earlier, we brought hoes and spades and rakes with us. The innocent children had a good time eating; the old folks complained and sobbed regrets about "such an Eve"; and the men gritted their teeth, said nothing, and swung their hoes. We didn't care how much noise and laughter the villagers made, we wouldn't hear it this far away. We sowed radishes. Then we clasped hands firmly and vowed to each other that we would work together with all our might. And it was this that happened to become our first step toward communal production and communal living.

Actually, having been ostracized, their ties with the villagers broken, freed from various rights and duties, the four families couldn't avoid strengthening their own bonds in order to make a living. For example, they helped each other weed paddy, going from one's fields to another's. It was once when Sensei and the others had gone to help weed the Imanishi fields in the western section that one of Mitani's kin called Imanishi aside and asked him, "What have you done wrong? If anybody speaks to you, it's a hundred-yen fine each time." That was how we first learned about the fine.

From time to time relatives came to us on the sly and asked us the reason for the ostracism. But we refused to discuss it, telling them as Sensei had instructed, "If that's what you want to know, you'd better go ask the village bosses instead of asking us."

When the Eve was past, we entered the November harvest season. In the village they were saying they would not lend the community-owned rice-huller to the four families. So the four families pooled their money in equal shares and bought a huller and a thresher of their own.

Once they had been refused the use of the huller even though they were members of the association, the four families requested repayment of their capital shares in the farmers' cooperative. It's not clear whether making the repayment would open such a financial gap that co-op management would be hurt, or whether it was just a matter of face; but the village went into an uproar. People came to offer compromises. They said they wanted to come to terms and settle the dispute without such formal action. The mayor came, the police came, and the head of the neighborhood association came. Finally even Seki Iwazō himself came. Sensei refused bluntly, telling them:

"This isn't the kind of dispute you 'compromise.' We didn't start any fight so there's no issue over which we have to come to terms. We've simply been ostracized for not having the right qualifications to be village citizens, and we're content to accept that. Instead of coming here you should go see those poor people in the village who are following the ostracism resolution without knowing anything about it, and ask them to tell you the origins of the reason for our being ostracized."

Each time people came to talk of compromise, Sensei's mother nervously begged him, "Masu, please settle it." But considerate as he was of his mother, Sensei hardened his heart and determined to carry out his convictions this time even though it meant going against her wishes. There was nothing else he could do if he was going to clean out a vile practice from the village. His agony must have been terrific; just watching him was painful for the rest of us.

The Seki faction wouldn't agree to make public the reason for the ostracism, so the deliberate attempts to compromise and reconcile the parties only ended in separating them again. Sensei and the four families grew all the more strong in their desire to take up communal production.

When the autumn collective harvest was done in December, the four families turned to baking charcoal. At first each family dug its own oven, cut its own wood and made it into charcoal. We helped each other only with the baking. But efficiency was poor this way. So from the second firing onward we collectivized thoroughly. That is, we baked everything in one oven on one hill. All we needed to do was to insert some sort of partition-marker in the wood in the oven, for convenience in sorting out each family's charcoal later. The situation had been the same at harvest time—even though you know it's right to share labor and fuel equally, when you get down to specific cases it becomes difficult, and we had trouble striking a fair balance. At any rate, collectivization began to make progress in one form and another.

As the new year dawned we had a suggestion—from nobody in particular—that we build a meeting place where all of us could gather at ease. For one thing, we also could get Ozaki Sensei to move there from Osaka. The site we chose was "Obatake," one of the Ozaki family's fields. It was on the border between Kasama and Yasuda, and was one of those lonely edge-of-the-village places where at night the foxes and badgers come and go. By the time the discussion was settled, it was May.

Plans were drawn in July, and on August 29th—by chance the death-day anniversary of Sensei's beloved daughter Masako—the ridgepole was raised. The next month, while the walls were still only roughed in, Sensei's family moved there. It was November when the house was finally finished. Sensei's family and mine had already been living together in Osaka, and because my husband's job was in Osaka, Sensei's wife and I arranged to take turns for a while coming out to help work on the Obatake house. People gossiped about it viciously as "wife-swapping," but by that time we no longer were paying attention to what they said.

The villagers had the Tenri Chapel as an assembly hall; now the four families had the Obatake house. All of us would gather there to talk things over, both before going out on collective labor and again after the work was done. Life was definitely more convenient. But it wasn't just a matter of convenience. Surely the greatest benefit was that Ozaki Sensei settled down for the first time and began to serve as fulltime leader. Not long after that we began to eat together, each bringing food from his home. Next we began to use the bath together.

Ritarō no longer could stand the way his relationships with his Kasama neighbors had gone sour. He said that since he was thinking of rebuilding anyway, he might as well move his buildings over by the Obatake house. First he pulled down a small shed and brought it over. And though it was only a crude beginning, this became our communal kitchen. This was in January, 1939.

Once we had a communal kitchen, the women and children also began to take their meals there regularly. Eight of us already were living in the house—Sensei, his wife (or myself), his wife's parents and their two children, my child, and Ritarō's child. At meals we were joined by four Yamanakas (husband, wife and two children); four Mitanis (same); and two Imanishis (husband and wife; the children couldn't come because their home was so far away in the western section). That made eighteen in all, ten adults and eight children. We managed the meals by pooling our money and our own produce.

My job was to cook and to take care of clothing for the eight children. Sensei had for some time eagerly urged people that, after taking a bath, they change from work clothes to *nemaki* [kimono used for lounging and sleeping]. This may seem trivial, but it was a great revolution in the clothing habits long standard in farm villages. So I thought I could at least see to it that the children had clean nemaki as often as possible.

One day when I began to wash the eight nemaki, my hand reached out and grabbed my own child's nemaki first. Once I noticed, I blinked in surprise. I'd had no bad intentions, no partiality. Without thinking about it at all, sometime or other I'd gotten into the habit of doing it that way. But if somebody else were to see it, well, it would look like selfish concern for my own child. If they said I lack impartiality, what could I say? Warning myself that anything like this is absolutely out when you're working and living communally, I let go of my child's nemaki and began washing them in order from the end of the rack. Much ado about nothing, maybe, but after all we didn't have a single pattern to follow then for the communal way of life we were starting. Only after we hit against various problems in reality would we begin to catch on. We always had to remember to be on the alert for the chance that what seemed to be a trifle might turn into a major issue that could rock the whole basis of our common life. For me this was a great discovery.

Again when I passed out the children's snacks I was thinking to myself, "It would be good if my child got the best pieces." The children had no way of knowing what I had in mind; innocent beings that they are, they were just yelling for joy. I came to my senses, and once again I felt that a mother's instinct was actually repulsive and could lead to mistakes here.

Ritarō began to pull down the old Ozaki home at the same time that he took down the small shed and made the temporary kitchen. That was on January 4, 1939. Although we did the rebuilding originally for the benefit of the Ozaki family, once it was done we saw that it nicely set the stage for a step forward from communal production to communal management. We had not planned from the start that things would go this way. Once we realized what was happening, it was "as unexpected as getting a colt from a calabash." All we had been thinking of was what we could do to make communal labor more efficient and economical, and what we could do to make an effective comeback from ostracism. That was the goal of our daily struggles, though no doubt deep in everybody's heart there was a feeling all along that if we were to work communally we ought to be together as much as possible. Then we wouldn't be lonely, and it would be equally convenient for all. That's why it wasn't unnatural at all that we began planning to move and rebuild all the homes in a way that would be convenient and at the same time suitable for communal life. And that's why when we moved one of the Ozaki main buildings—the one called the Storehouse—it became our headquarters. It could have been pure chance that the building stood on a spot called *yon-kembō* but I think that that must have some meaning. [She writes *yonkembō* with three graphs that mean "four family temple." She is punning upon a place-name whose original meaning is obscure, although I would guess that it probably meant something like "four rod dike."]

The women of the four families took charge of the kitchen by turns, each doing the cooking for a week at a time. A woman who until then had done nothing but work in the fields like an ox now was responsible for meals for everybody, and she had to use her imagination like a city wife. No matter how busy her job got at times, in one sense it was a delight and gave her something worth living for as a woman. That meant more than a man could imagine.

The ordinary farm bride has to work like a machine or a draft animal while she tries to bear up under the ugly tradition that allows her mother-in-law to enjoy tormenting her. The only consolation she has is her hope for the future; if she can take it, in time the family property will become her property as well, and when the positions change she will sit in the mother-in-law's seat and her life will be a little easier.

All the women of the four families were alike on this point. Under communal labor and communal cooking, their standing as women who had come to the village as brides and had proved they could take it suddenly became shaky, so it isn't strange that they were caught up in uncertainty. Also, unlike the men, their standing had no direct connection to the ostracism.

However, as each wife set aside her field clothes and tied on a white apron, and tried her hand at cooking for a group without the meddlesome interference of a mother-in-law, she found a change, a gain, and an excitement that she hadn't expected. Once we had tried it, we found it could even be fun.

Every day the duty cook kept a kitchen day-book. Women who had come as brides were now recording figures and lists on paper, holding pens that for a long time they'd had no chance to hold, in knobby hands roughened by sickles and hoes.

As we were doing these things we definitely gave birth to what I'd call a new style of life. Slowly we had begun to change—especially the women—and to feel that we'd be far better off finding satisfaction in our daily communal life than fretting about family wealth and so on in a future that we couldn't count on anyway.

But surely there was no reason to expect that everything would go smoothly. I have to admit that the others could not (any more easily than I could) break away from bonds to dependents or from the instinctive selfishness you feel for kinsmen; and that there was an unseen suspiciousness and sense of competition at work among us. For example the duty cook would bring her own child to stay with her in the kitchen, and even if she didn't go so far as to make anything special for the child, she might leave her own serving untouched and give it to him. We hadn't particularly talked about it, but it turned out that every one of us was doing the same thing. And we were jealously suspicious about the partiality that other mothers might be showing toward their children. The children themselves caught on too, and each of them began to wait impatiently for his mother to take the kitchen duty. Under these conditions communal life would not work. If we ignored them, we probably would end up separating again.

At this point Sensei suggested that the children trade off and sleep with somebody else's parents. At first glance it looked like a good idea, but in fact a child who happened to wake in the night and realize that the person sleeping next to him was not his mother but "some auntie or other" would start bawling and wouldn't stop. The temporary mother-for-the-night was really in a fix. But no matter how angry it made her, when she realized that her child probably was annoying some other mother too, she just had to set aside her feelings and do something to quiet the one with her. As these experiences accumulated, the idea of playing favorites with your own child simply faded away.

Then some of the duty cooks gave up making the yam gruel that is traditional in Yamato, and began serving rice frequently. The elders grumbled uneasily:

"If we live on rice, our families aren't going to last three years." "I've lived on gruel for a long, long time; you tell me to give it up now and I get scared. How will we manage?" [They feared that meals were becoming too luxurious. Rice was their cash-income crop. They preferred to eat it sparingly, and subsist on cheaper fare, in order to increase their income.]

The elders wanted to take their complaints to their friends in the village, but they couldn't. As usual, the villagers wouldn't have any part of it, and if any of us seemed about to speak to them, they would turn their backs sharply.

The duty cook was responsible for feeding not only humans but oxen. We had also begun communal cattle care. The men took turns each day in the barn. Part of the Storehouse was divided into four cattle pens. Until we had this building, each day when communal work in the fields was over, each man led his own ox home, fed it and cleaned its pen.

In the early stages the men on cattle duty were just like the women on kitchen duty: each favored his own ox, giving it extra feed or being more careful about cleaning its pen. But he couldn't avoid having a guilty conscience as he did it. The men say that one day when one of them spoke out and they realized that they all were worried about it, they had mixed feelings of strangeness and shame.

Sensei suggested that we sell off the four oxen in order to do away with these feelings. The four families agreed, sold the oxen and bought different ones instead. That way the notion of which ox was whose no longer applied. For good or bad all of them had to be treated with equal care. This was how the oxen came to be our first common property. It was in July of 1939.

As I said before, we had pooled our money and bought machinery for hulling and threshing. But that was more a form of cooperative use than of common ownership, and until the Storehouse was built the machines were kept in a shed on one of the Yamanaka fields. Once we had the communal workshop, of course, we put the machines into it. On rainy days the members gathered in the workshop, and joking as they worked, they made straw boots and sandals. Also, we could then do evening craftwork without having to go to each home as we had before.

We had originally partitioned a storeroom into four bins, one for each family, and distributed the crops among them. Sensei laughed at this: "You are sorting these out equally, but if the share which one of the families gets isn't enough, or if one family can't give as much labor as the others, then what? Does that negate communal labor, or will the other three families simply add more to help out? If we're going to forget our own wants and help each other, we don't have any business sorting things into four precise piles."

The members all said "Of course." And except for rice we brought everything under communal control, without partitions, and everybody was free to carry home as much as he needed. The need to carry food home gradually decreased as communal cooking was done on a more complete scale.

But rice remained the exception. Since rice is the one thing a farmer could readily change into cash, it couldn't be pooled, we thought. So we divided the rice room into four sections and were strict about private control. It wasn't unreasonable. If you follow the thinking of a farmer about the special significance of rice, you see that he regards communal control of rice as being the next thing to communal control of his wealth and of his family itself; and inevitably he's opposed. Sensei said again and again:

"If you all haven't the guts to go on helping each other in any and every way, then how about apologizing to the village now and getting the ostracism removed?"

The four families said they'd die before they'd do that. "Well then," Sensei told them, "if you feel that way about apologizing to the village, a little thing like putting all your rice into one bin isn't anything at all, is it?" This came up a number of times, and in the end we eventually were able to bring rice under communal control too.

After that came the question of communal bathing. During the day the men and women would work together, but when bath time came they separated, and by farm village custom the women would not enter the bath until all the men were finished. This practice wasted time and was uneconomical with fuel, so we changed our habit and let anybody who was free, man or woman, use the bath. Before long the men also began to enter without embarrassment while women were in the tub, and in a very natural way we developed a practice of group bathing. [American stereotypes of the Japanese portray them as addicted to group bathing. In fact it is uncommon except at resort hotels and hot-springs. The family bathtub rarely is large enough to permit it, and twentieth century public bathhouses usually are sex-segregated. Furthermore, within a family the order of precedence in entering the bath is a measure of status—in general, males and older persons are first.]

Next there was a question of dividing the rooms. The Storehouse had a three-foot-wide hall down the center, with each side divided into five rooms of six-mat size. The Ozaki family's belongings had been moved into the five rooms on the south side, and on the north side we had a crowd that included Yamanaka and his wife, the Imanishis, all the children, Sensei, his wife's parents, myself, and six or seven other people related to us. It was so jammed we would match each other to see who'd have to sleep in the closets. We called ourselves the four families, but at some point we had become eight families. The Imanishis too, who had been standing alone against the pressures of ostracism in the western section, finally couldn't take it any more and moved in. They left their belongings at Mitani's house.

The same thing happened with the Yamanakas. Their household included an old couple, and they positively refused to go along with communal meals and communal management. They rented a corner cottage from another family and lived by themselves. The father died there, and afterwards the mother convinced herself that we had stolen her family's wealth, and she went around publicly denouncing Sensei.

We added the Imanishi chests to the five rooms where

the Ozaki belongings were stored, then the chests of the Yamanakas and the Mitanis too. That is, common use of the chests and the clothing began spontaneously. It wasn't that we had planned originally to combine our clothing. The thought had merely arisen that putting things together would be handy and there'd be no waste. For example, in the first chest we put all the men's dress over-kimono, in the second chest the women's going-out kimono, in the third all of our everyday clothes.

One day in September Yukimura, one of the influential villagers, told Mitani, "I'm not giving you any more water for your paddy." Since Yukimura's paddy was higher, its water was supposed to be shared with Mitani's below. There are times when water is short. But farmer ethics won't excuse this kind of conduct no matter how much you try to blame it on a water shortage. When they heard about it, Sensei and the four families quickly had a carpenter from a nearby village bring a measuring rod and set it up in Mitani's paddy. This was standard preparation for erecting a building.

Yukimura apparently looked down from his paddy and wondered what they were trying to do. His scheme to make trouble for Mitani seemed to have gone haywire, and he looked a little disappointed.

Soon after that a terrific rain fell. It meant that he would have to let the water dammed up in his paddy run out into Mitani's field below. Yukimura came and said it was "all right to draw water," though what he really was thinking was "I'm asking you to please draw water or I'll be in a bad spot." But this time it was Mitani's turn to be stubborn. "Oh, that's all right," he said, "you absolutely shouldn't let any water down. I don't need any water." In other words Mitani completely threw away the water rights for that paddy.

After that the Mitani family decided to move down

from the hilltop. We promised not to tear down the Mitani home itself but to leave it as a spare dwelling. Mitani decided they would move when the rice ears were out in his paddy. The moving was a tremendous chore since we couldn't get any help and had to manage it by ourselves, somehow finding time between bouts of work on the dozen and a half acres of paddy the four families owned. Every morning at two Sensei would take the lead, carrying rooftiles and lumber from the Mitani buildings. Besides, we were doing craftwork into the night, so that our bodies didn't get a chance to completely recover from being tired. The village watched with amazement, but thanks to our determination in the face of the ostracism we didn't feel sleepy and didn't realize how tired we were. It *is* true that willpower makes strength. Not one of us took sick.

On New Year's Day of 1940 we moved into our new building while its walls were still only rough-plastered. We called it the Cookhouse. It was 24 feet wide and 100 feet long, a pretty good-sized structure. We made this our living quarters and used the Storehouse in fact as well as in name as a storehouse.

The Cookhouse had four bedrooms on the second floor, and four bedrooms and two guest rooms downstairs. In addition it had a bath, washroom, pantry, kitchen, 20 x 30-foot wood-floored dining room, and a dirt-floored dining room. We took advantage of the water level and ran pipes to the kitchen, bath and washroom. It cost us two thousand yen, but in a farm village in those days such civilized facilities were a novelty. We heard that the villagers were spreading rumors that "if they could put in facilities like that they must've gotten money from Russia."

But in fact the only reason why we had enough money to build it was because we didn't celebrate Midsummer or New Year's, and we didn't take any days off. We moved on New Year's Day, then we pulled down the small dwelling at Yamanaka's and brought it over. And under the cold sky of

January 4th we kneaded clay for the walls. A month later we had finished. The building had two rooms on the second floor and two downstairs, all of them usable as bedrooms.

And this was how from 1939 into 1940 we completed laying the main foundations for our communal life.

CHAPTER SEVEN

To build an imperial shrine

Seki Iwazō and his conservative power elite never let up on us. As we struggled to organize our communal life, and somehow got it to working, the pressures not only didn't slack off, they grew worse and more subtle. The Seki gang went to the police again, spilling fantasies about how we must be communists because we were tearing down or abandoning the houses we had inherited, and had gone to live together. One of their maneuvers involved the building of an imperial shrine.

It was near the third Eve after we were ostracized from the village, toward the end of September, 1939. In those days Emperor-worship was being urged upon the people more forcefully than ever, and every school was eager to have a shrine or a repository in which to display the Emperor's photograph. Mr. Matsuyama, principal of the Kasama primary school, assembled his pupils and told them, "Soon the Eve will be here, and those who are participating in the festival may take a vacation. But those who will not participate must come to school as usual and work ahead on their lessons."

By custom, school would be out for everybody during a village-wide festival, so that children as well as adults could properly invite guests and be invited in turn. Families that celebrated the Eve would take great pains about everything, repairing their houses and laying money aside well in advance. A temporary market would be opened in the village, and fishmongers would come out from the city; everybody would have one of the few real feasts of the year. For the children in particular it was a pleasure for which there could be no substitutes. Nevertheless, the principal said some would have to come to school. They knew perfectly well that he meant our children. The rest of them hooted at our kids, "Yaaa . . . we're going to the festival and we'll have fishpaste and squid. We'll show you!"

Badly hurt by what the principal had told them, whether he had been deliberate or just careless, they came crying home. Sensei was unusually furious. "All right then," he said, "I'll see that principal tomorrow and have some words with him about it."

We parents also pinned great hopes on Sensei's counterattack, thinking it might bring some revenge for the humiliation the children always suffered in school. Next morning we all went to one of our paddies beside the school and harvested rice as we anxiously waited for the principal. He came on a bicycle. Sensei, in his work boots, chased after him right into the school building. We watched him with the kind of look you'd give to a brave soldier setting off for the front.

When he finally came back we sat around him in a circle in the paddy. "Well, how did it go? What did the principal say?" Without replying directly to the impatient parents, Sensei was lost in thought for a moment, then raised his head abruptly and said, "I agreed that we'd donate an imperial repository. I told him, 'Because of what you said, our kids all came home in tears, and the others made fun of them.' And he looked mad and said, 'Mr. Ozaki, settle your differences with the village; settle your differences.' So I pounded on his desk and shouted at him, 'You bastard! We can't trust our kids to a rat like you. We'll send them to another school. You aren't supposed to be putting your oar into village affairs. If you're an educator, act like an educator. When you educate children you should have an attitude that's as disinterested as water!'

"I must have had such a fierce look on my face as I yelled at him that he got panicky. 'Mr. Ozaki, Mr. Ozaki, really now, let's not get angry. I had heard that your younger brother was going to donate an imperial repository to the school, and then that sometime or other you told him not to. That's why I am asking you to settle your differences.' But that just made me mad again. 'Who said he'd donate a repository? When? Well! Tell me!' That old principal was shaking like a leaf. 'Mr. Ozaki, if I mentioned his name it would cost me my head. Please, let's keep it quiet.' He put his hand to his neck and looked like he was going to cry. When I saw that, I thought, well, he's really in sad shape."

What the principal said about a younger brother refers to this: Sensei has a younger brother who was adopted as heir to a wealthy Osaka household. The village bosses had asked him if he wouldn't donate a repository to the primary school. But soon after that we were ostracized, and the talk of donations died out. Because they were going to lose face, the Seki faction in their desperation must have lied to the principal and told him that Sensei had forbidden the donation.

Sensei thought it over. With a flourish he said to the principal, "We will donate that imperial repository. My younger brother had been going to do it, but he's already a resident of Osaka. Village problems should be taken care of by village people, after all."

And so it was decided, and none of us objected. The price was a thousand yen, a huge sum considering our standard of living and the cost of things in those days. We had to squeeze it out somehow, so we completely changed our style of life. Our income was limited and couldn't be increased much at one swoop, so all we could do was cut down on food and clothing. Nobody grumbled, though. Several of us saved money by not wearing rubber-soled *tabi* or boots, and when we weren't out working in the fields we made ourselves straw sandals. Every day after they came home from school, the primary schoolers and even the first graders helped make straw sandals. The ones in higher primary school braided straw ropes. The sandals they were able to make wouldn't last us a week, so they were hard pressed to keep up with the demand. The adults, when they realized what harm Seki's trickery was causing, vowed to get revenge. And of course the parents couldn't look on indifferently when they saw their children going off to school in straw sandals instead of shoes.

Eventually we managed to get that thousand yen together. They say that principal Matsuyama took the check and hurried over to the township office saying, "This is great! Great!" And no doubt it was something: in those days you could keep an adult supplied with rice for a year for eighty yen.

About ten days later all of us were out harvesting rice in the Nakanishi paddy, one of Yamanaka's fields. Across the dike came Seki Yūzō, one of Iwazō's relatives, with five or six of the other teachers. Nobody had spoken to us publicly since the ostracizing, so we watched with suspicion as Yūzō drew close.

"You are to donate a repository, but because of the war, it's impossible to get concrete and steel, so it appears that instead we will have to have an imperial shrine made completely out of wood." He just happened to have come from inspecting the imperial shrine at the Takai primary school in Uda county. It was a one-sided change of plans, and we would have been out of our minds not to get angry about it. But to keep us from talking back, Sensei asked him, "That imperial shrine, how much would it take?" According to Yūzō, it would need a roof of cypress bark; the lumber must be unblemished cypress; and the doors must have a metal imperial chrysanthemum crest—all together it would cost 3500 or 3600 yen. All of us were stunned.

Principal Matsuyama had trusted only the Seki faction and had despised us without any good reason. But once he heard that we would donate a repository he changed his mind, and suddenly was friendly and happy. Seki and his group couldn't take that calmly. They didn't dare openly object to the building of a repository, so they arranged to demand the shrine instead.

Everybody held his breath. All eyes were focused on Sensei. Whatever he said, his words would carry tons of weight. Not hesitating a bit, he said, "All right, then we'll donate a shrine!"

One imperial shrine: 3500 yen—the price of 170 sacks of rice. What kept us going was our determination that we wouldn't knuckle under to *them*. Once we'd beat our chests and promised, we absolutely had to prove we could do it no matter how painful it was for us, even if we ended up chewing stones. When you think about it, the Eve, which ought to be such a happy affair, brought us our share of problems and pains. It really was our unlucky day.

The Kasama principal took the Kurozaki principal with him when he went to inspect the shrine at the Takai school. On the way back they stopped in at our place. The Kasama principal was acting as though it all had come about thanks to his efforts, and he was blowing hot air at his colleague. Sensei was secretly disgusted; and when he saw how utterly downcast the Kurozaki principal was he felt sorry for him. He consoled him by promising that we'd get together *five thousand* yen somehow, that 3500 of it would go to Kasama and the remainder to Kurozaki as a starter fund for their own shrine. Then when he noticed a look of dissatisfaction on the Kasama principal's face, Sensei proposed the following.

For some decades the Kasama school had had to pay rent for the land it was using; if that land were exchanged for some nearby fields that we owned, we'd charge no rent. The condition would be that the money previously used for rent would hereafter be applied to the upkeep of the shrine we were donating. Sensei already was looking into the future and thinking about the cost of repairing the new structure.

The Kurozaki principal said, "With fifteen hundred yen from you as a starter, we'll get other donations from our alumni and surely be able to put together enough for a shrine." Sensei stopped him, "Let's have none of that; no combined funds. We ourselves will definitely get all the money for you one way or another, so I want you to start construction with the fifteen hundred. If we drop out before it's finished, I want you to tear it all down and start over with a new donor."

That was how we came to promise imperial shrines to two schools. Not that the doing was easy. Even if we sold all our rice off the paddies and kept none to eat ourselves, it still wouldn't bring in enough cash. So we borrowed money with some real estate as security, and we cut down our standard of living even further.

The foundations for the Kasama shrine were laid in an easterly corner of the schoolyard. We spent more than a month at it. Stone-masons gathered the stone, cut them, and supervised the laying. The villagers were rounded up to do "patriotic labor" for it. Of course Seki and his gang weren't happy about doing that kind of labor, but since it was for an imperial shrine they couldn't oppose it and instead interfered on the sly. We gave tea and cakes to the school children when they carried stones, and sometimes we furnished meals for the villagers on the labor crews; we also gave aid of many other sorts.

About five months after the Eve we saw the completed shrine. The imperial chrysanthemum crest glittered brilliantly; it seemed completely above and beyond our village feud.

A team came from the prefectural office to make arrangements for accepting the donation of the shrine. They said it was standard procedure to record the name of the donors' representative. Sensei insisted that we didn't have a representative, that all of us had contributed wholeheartedly. But they wouldn't allow us to record all our names because the document didn't have enough room. Somebody suggested making up a fictitious name, but Sensei said, "Let's have the mayor do it. Mayor, will you be our representative?" He was caught off guard and was a little flustered; but when he thought about it, his name would be preserved for posterity, and what better for his reputation? So it was an official acceptance like none before: he gave the shrine in his name as representative and accepted it in his name as mayor. With that the documentary part of it was settled.

There was a dedication ceremony, of course, but none of us went. Considering the atmosphere in the village at the time, there surely would have been friction. We had one of Sensei's Osaka parishioners go as our stand-in. Seki Iwazō gave a speech as spokesman for the township council, and it stirred up a buzz because he said of us, "On many points they are not in harmony with the Imperial Way. . . ." Our man came right back and told us that one of the township councilmen said some wild things. Sensei was again boiling mad and took himself off to the ceremony.

"Why should people who are not in harmony with the Imperial Way donate an imperial shrine? And why should a township councilman accept an imperial shrine donated by people not in harmony with the Imperial Way? And another thing—the police who heard him speak about people not in harmony with the Imperial Way, why didn't they arrest us all? Well? I want an answer right now! If it isn't the right answer, I'll knock this shrine down today, here and now!"

He seemed to be glaring right through the lines of

guests. It goes without saying that the mayor and councilmen turned pale and choked up. If the affair was brought out in public, they wouldn't stand a chance of defending themselves. In desperation they said to Sensei, "Look, we've invited so many official guests, let's be peaceable about it for now and we'll find a solution in good time." Under the circumstances all he could do was cool his anger.

Afterwards the township council met and the mayor accused Seki of improper conduct. Seki couldn't help but agree to a retraction. And some days later in hope of burying the hatchet we invited about twenty people—the mayor, the councilmen, the principals—to a drinking party.

As the party progressed, the Kurozaki principal suggested (it was his idea) that before everybody finished drinking, he would lead us in a *banzai* for the Emperor. So far, so good; but then he also called for a *banzai* for the shrine donors. Everybody jumped up and joined in. They sat down again, some going on drinking and others starting to eat, when Seki Iwazō, sitting in the center, said in a drunken, hoarse voice, "Principal, you're out of order!" And he began to shout, "grab him! grab him!"

Naturally as far as the principal was concerned, he hadn't thought he was doing wrong. Anyway, what he'd done was nothing compared to Seki's insult during an official ceremony. It had all been in good fun. Maybe Seki couldn't think clearly with his sake-soggy mind; and maybe because they were so used to submitting blindly to Seki, everybody got up as Seki kept shouting to hold the principal and beat him, and it looked as though there was going to be a real free-for-all. The principal crouched meekly in a corner of the veranda. Men were stripping to the waist, doubling their fists, one big mob of drunks yelling on and on. Sensei grabbed a huge platter, jumped up and slammed it against a sill. It flew into bits.

"Everybody sit!" His shout had amazing results. In a moment they were as silent as if he'd thrown cold water over them.

"Listen to me. I haven't had a drop to drink. Getting drunk on just a little sake and then starting a brawl—is that how councilmen act when they're handling township affairs? Seki! Listen well! What do you suppose this party is for? Don't you understand the feelings of people when they not only don't pick a fight about your insults but even invite you to a drinking party like this? The principal's little joke . . . what of it? Wasn't he just showing how happy he was after he'd had a few drinks? Even if somebody else were to complain about it, considering how you've acted what you really ought to do is to put in a good word for him, shouldn't you? Instead you take the lead and holler to grab him and beat him. You're scum! A viper who spreads his poison in society the way you do can't be left alone, so I'll take over the gods' duty and straighten you out. Come here! Rats like you won't stop until they are beaten to death, so come on!"

What a tremendous scowl there was on his face! It was the first time we'd seen him act so violently. The drunks looked on blankly, struck dumb. Seki took to his heels and fled.

The shrine for the Kasama school was donated in the spring of 1940, and the shrine for the Kurozaki school was completed the following year. Although it wasn't easy for us to pay for both shrines by ourselves, we managed to cover the cost of everything down to the final celebration banquets. Not only that, but we also got caught in a situation in which we had to buy some land for the Kurozaki school and a 24-horsepower gasoline pump for Asakura township.

The township mayor had acted as our nominal representative when the shrine donation was officially recorded. As a result, his goodwill towards us grew stronger. That, of course, angered Seki and his gang, and they retaliated with the pump affair.

The township council had unanimously approved buying the pump. But when Seki later argued that there was no way to raise the money for it, the council reversed its decision. The mayor was in a dilemma, since he already had ordered the pump. At that time the Kurozaki shrine was under construction and we were there seeing how it was coming. One of the councilmen came from the meeting and said to Sensei, "The mayor's in a bind and he'll have to resign; can't you do something for him?"

Sensei went straight to the meeting. The whole council was maneuvering against our representative. A pale-looking mayor said, "The prefecture won't excuse this; I'll have to cut my guts out."

"You've got pretty weak guts," said Sensei, "but is that any reason to kill yourself? Let us help you out." He meant that we'd take over and buy the pump, since it already had been ordered.

But 4500 yen for a pump was another big sum of money. We had nothing left over after building the two shrines. So we had to sell off almost two acres of paddy to raise the cash. Because of that the mayor's reputation was saved, and we owned a pump even though we didn't want one. In an about face, the council asked us to sign over the pump to them. Even Sensei wasn't so gullible as to go along with that; in fact he scolded them, "You didn't buy the pump even though you'd already agreed to, because you decided the township didn't need one. So why do you say now that we should sign the pump over to you?"

Logically he was right, and the councilmen had no comeback. But he wasn't being spiteful. "I don't suppose we'll have any use for this pump. But we aren't going to let go of it ever, even if it falls to pieces. Almost two paddy's worth of our ancestors' blood runs through that pump. However, Asakura township will be in trouble if it doesn't have a pump. We won't sign it over to you, but we will lend it to you. And we'll lend it free."

In the four years since the ostracizing we had met one

bitter test after another, and with each one our bonds tightened. People had gotten into the habit of calling our commune "the Shinkyō hamlet" and our group "the Shinkyō people." They didn't cancel the ostracism, but they no longer were able to deny that we existed.

And although the Seki faction's power still was strong, we had never given in to it. In case after case their scheming had failed right before the eyes of the village. To that extent they had accumulated losses of face, and their despotism no longer operated as it once had. We had even come to pity the man Seki.

In the fall of 1940, when we heard that Seki's wife was ill and that they were having trouble getting in their harvest, Sensei took our Shinkyō threshing machine and went over to help. In one day we threshed more than two and one-half acres of paddy for them. We took lunches so they wouldn't have to feed us. And to cheer up Seki, who was downcast because of his wife, we even lured him over to Shinkyō for supper.

CHAPTER EIGHT

We emigrate to Manchuria

Wartime living conditions grew more and more severe each day. You couldn't escape their influence even in villages, away from the cities where people were under daily pressure for military production. Quite the opposite: the forced supply system for farm products became strict. Grades of paddy were established, each family's fields were surveyed, and supply quotas were enforced officially.

Seki Iwazō, as you might expect, used the supply system to bring pressure on Shinkyō. That is, our quota was made very unfairly heavy. His explanation was that, "Since you are making your crop collectively, there's no doubt but what your yields are good. That's why you're in the extra high quality grade." Without even surveying our fields they flatly certified us as extra high grade. Call it fame if you want—but if that's fame, what a burden!

Before the harvest of 1942 the quotas became absolute, and no one had a chance to object. If you didn't fill your quota you were immediately threatened with "severe measures," and could even be cited for treason. We heard that at one Kasama farm Seki went with the police to search the granary, said it had too much rice in it, and had the police beat the head of the household in front of the villagers. Afterward, we were told, the man went to Seki's house and said, "Please show me your family's granary:

if there's no rice in it, then I'll gladly consent to deliver all mine to the supply system." But Seki stubbornly refused. Some days later when Sensei asked him, "Why didn't you show him your granary?," Seki came back with the illogical reply, "Suppose I showed the rice in my granary— it would be bad if there was too much and bad if there was too little." I heard that the beaten man was so bitter about it that he was saying he'd hang himself at the gate of that terrible Seki, but he soon died from illness.

Before long the village got its rations of rice in return from the supply system, but Shinkyō refused to take any, on grounds that if a farmer took ration-rice it was the same as if a soldier on the battlefield turned his back to the enemy. One day I went, as Sensei had ordered, to coax Seki into getting the whole village to stop taking rations. "As Sensei told you the other day, if you'll refuse the rations, Shinkyō will donate all its wheat to the village. Then if the village collects everybody's grain and potatoes, and opens a community kitchen, we'll surely get along, won't we?"

Finally I added, "If you're not going to listen to us, there's talk of developing Manchuria with people from Kagawa prefecture, and we think we'll all go there." But Seki showed no interest. All I could do was withdraw silently.

I don't exactly remember any more when the talk of moving to Manchuria was brought up. Somebody mentioned it when we were chatting as usual at the Obatake house. When they heard it, the heads of the four families very simply said, "Shall we?" and agreed to it. Listening at their side, I was caught up with the idea and said, "That would be great, wouldn't it?" And so the decision was made in an extremely casual way. But it goes without saying that you don't carry a decision through without friction when it involves moving every member of a number of

95

families a thousand miles to the continent. After that, every time we came together we talked about moving. Of course some argued against it, and some urged caution. We agreed and we disagreed and we thrashed it out fairly. There was a feeling, especially among the old folk, that no matter how the local people treated them they wanted to stay here walking the land of their ancestors' graves. Others contradicted. "If we stay here, have we got anything to look forward to? All the unspeakable humiliation and oppression since we were ostracized—can we expect that to die down? It's bad enough for the adults; what's going to happen to the children?"

Right at this time—perhaps by chance—there came a great change in Sensei's life and in mine. That is, his wife left him and remarried another man. It seems that she

Kotoè

had always doubted his feelings, that her jealousy and suspicion had grown fierce and she'd fought with him; and
when talk of Manchuria came up she decided she just
couldn't follow him any more. My husband also divorced
me and soon married another woman. I was quite surprised
at how skillfully it was done—it could only have been
planned in advance. The grounds were the same as those
given by Sensei's wife. And so Sensei and I each broke
away from fifteen years of married life and became single
in middle age.

The Shinkyō advance party that left in the latter part
of May, 1943, had a total strength of eleven persons. Sensei
went, of course, and with him Ozaki Ritarō, Yamanaka
Hisajirō, Imanishi Tokuichi, Yamanaka Itarō, Yamanaka
Takejirō, Ozaki Ri'ichi, Nishimura Kin'ichirō, Yamanaka
Kimiyo, Yamanaka Zenshichi, and myself. After only a
month Ritarō, Hisajirō and Zenshichi came back to the village to trade places with another group, and Sensei and I
came back to lead the second party over.

We made ready to go to Manchuria again late in June
of the following year. The second party was to go when the
paddy had been put in order. The party was made up mostly
of children. There were three adults: Sensei, myself, and
Yamanaka Masae. Then came sixteen-year-old Imanishi
Akiko as children's leader, with all the rest of them primary-
school age or younger: Imanishi Kiyoichi (second grade),
Imanishi Masa'aki (first), Mitani Chōjūrō (sixth), Yamanaka Isamu (sixth), Yamanaka Haku (fourth), Mitani Ki-
kuko (fourth), Mitani Masuichi (third), Mitani Wao (first),
and Imanishi Shizu and Yamanaka Kaoru who weren't even
in school yet. It was truly a team of young pioneers.

Those lucky enough to have one or both parents with
them in Manchuria were the Yamanaka brothers Isamu and
Haku (father Itarō, mother Masae) and the three Imanishis,
Kiyoichi, Masa'aki and Shizu (father Tokuichi). Their

97

mother Yurie was to stay behind, however, until work in the paddies was done. The four Mitani children and Yamanaka Kaoru had to leave both parents behind.

It was a sad and miserable parting and we'll always remember it. The small children had suitably small rucksacks on their backs; the bigger ones carried enough food for a week's trip. The parents saw them off as far as Haibara station. It was one of those railway partings where you never know if it may be the last time you'll see each other in this life. Tears shone in the eyes of the three mothers. Everybody was straining to hold back tears, so they had rather angry looks on their faces. Their gloom clouded up the outside of the train windows. If I had tried to say anything, the tears would have burst out, so I silently bowed my head to each of them one by one.

The children acted as though they were off for a picnic, and as a parting present to their parents they enthusiastically sang the Manchurian Pioneer Song we'd taught them.

> Our sturdy bodies burnt to a continental color,
> we flame with pioneer pride.
> The sun rises—it's a wide world—for pioneers.
> We'll do it! Watch our spirits soar!

Even after the train started they went on singing. Their voices flowed through the car and finally disappeared beyond the windows.

Taikozan—that was the name of the rural station where we arrived after a week's travel. There were raw marks from projectiles here and there around the station, which told of severe fighting here during the Manchurian Incident. Inside, Manchurians who had been waiting by the tracks for many days to get onto a train were sprawled on hideously filthy blankets and bundles. We passed through the crowd of garlic-reeking people and went out into the station plaza. On the wide plain some Manchurian girls picked a grass called *kamadogaeshi* for us. The manager of the

Development Group, who had come to meet us, told us that this grass was being picked and eaten because of the food shortage.

The first impression that struck me in Imperial Manchuria was the sad sight of the Manchurians. I was amazed to see people on the roads so desperate for food that they were eating raw cucumbers. There were men walking around selling water from teakettles. Whether you looked left or right, all anybody had to wear was black clothes.

After bumping along in a wagon for more than an hour we finally came to our village, Huangchia. To be exact it was known as the Minami Rikugo Development Group, Huangchia village, Daian prefecture, Kin region, Manchukuo. Its home village was in Minami Rikuka county in Kagawa prefecture, back in the Japanese islands; their advance party had moved here two years earlier. They had about a hundred people and had called their families over and gotten a temporary village organization going.

However, although the advance party were all agreed when they came that they would operate collectively, once they had called their families over they began shifting to individual operations. When Mr. O, one of the Group, happened to go back to the homeland, he stopped at Shinkyō and said to us, "In Manchuria you have to work communally or you won't make a go of it. Couldn't we get somebody from Shinkyō to come lead us in communal living?" Actually, this was what had motivated us; and once we had decided that all of us would move to Manchuria, we first changed our residence-of-record to the Group's home village in Kagawa.

Group organization consisted of four teams, and Shinkyō was assigned to team one. The team included Shinkyō and four other families, plus some bachelors. The houses were scattered over the landscape, two families to each. Shinkyō was assigned to one of them.

"We never have anything but sorghum to eat, but

since it's the first day here for you Shinkyō people, we'll have rice," said an old woman in the community kitchen. She prepared dry-field rice with salted salmon and made lunch for us.

The kitchen was in the center of the community. Next to it was the Group office, which housed the staff: a former schoolteacher as leader, a former *sushi* [raw fish delicatessen] shopkeeper as manager, a police marshal, and an agricultural advisor.

Each team had its team captain, and Mr. O was captain of team one. He was no end of help to us in getting settled. His pet idea seemed to be that if things went on the way they were, the Group would fade away from lack of active leadership; and so, as the prefectural officials also had suggested, there should be changes in the staff, and operating methods should be rebuilt from the ground up. Mr. O was a disabled veteran who could swing a hoe despite his injured hands; he also spoke Manchurian fairly well. Since he had been responsible for the Group's external affairs, he seemed to be on close terms with the prefectural officials. Confronted by Mr. O with these major issues on the very first day, Ozaki Sensei was completely lost in thought.

The next day, as a way of getting acquainted with the Group, we made them a pork dinner. Pork was considered the greatest treat of all in that area. We bought two hogs and treated all hundred members. We asked about the two Manchurians who were grooming the horses. Mr. O explained that they were coolies employed by the group. They had come to the station to meet us the day before. When Sensei said to Mr. O that the coolies also should be given some of the pork, Mr. O shook his head and wouldn't hear of it under any circumstances. "You can't do that. It isn't good to pamper these coolies." We had come to Manchuria believing the official slogan about "five peoples peacefully cooperating," so it was a real shock to find that the cooperation consisted of crude and crass discrimination. It was hard to take: we wondered where we had come.

About a week after we arrived, the entire Group met with Sensei. The leader—who knew the gossip about his being replaced—stayed in a corner in the office, paying no attention to his duties. Sensei proposed that the most sensible thing would be to have Mr. O take over the office of manager. If the Group got back on its feet, there'd be no need to replace the leader. "Even if you're not formally designated as manager, if you're really thinking of Group welfare, won't you move into the office and be counsel to the leader?"

There wasn't any reason for the members to disagree; and even if Mr. O was unhappy about not sitting in the leader's chair, it was difficult for him to attack Sensei's argument. So he agreed. But Sensei's proposal didn't end there. Since Mr. O would lose his good standing in the Group if he had his own team too much on his mind, said Sensei, we ought to formally choose a new team captain to succeed him. Caught off guard, Mr. O seemed quite shaken; some members appeared to be thinking, "This Ozaki wants to be captain himself." But Sensei at once added, "I nominate Yamada as captain of team one."

When the meeting was over, the leader came to Sensei and thanked him. And after that Sensei rapidly became popular with the members. Clothing or housing matters, or anything they found difficult to mention directly to the staff, even the most trifling complaints, were brought to Sensei.

Seeds of various sorts were distributed, and planting began. The garden plots around the houses were circled by sorghum stalks as windbreaks. There we planted cucumbers, eggplant, tomatoes, and watermelons. Then we went out to plant sorghum in the huge fields. We piled seeds and tools on the wagons and rode on top of it all. We recklessly cut through fields the Manchurians already had finished planting. Running a horse through somebody else's fields would be unthinkable in the homeland, but it was done here, as the staff explained to us, "because that way you naturally cut yourself a road."

The soothing continental spring breeze stroked our cheeks. In fields near and far we could see Manchurians in the midst of planting or even weeding already. They would stand perfectly straight, and into a bag hung from the neck they would thrust the right hand and pull out some seed. Twisting the thumb between index and middle fingers they would move ahead planting exactly three grains each at the same distance and same speed. By contrast we dropped seed at a running clip into the furrows the horses had cut. Planting seed? You might better call it throwing away seed!

Although we hung the seed bag from our necks too, our bag hung from the left shoulder downward to the right, and in front there was a thing like an upside-down trumpet. Its tip was divided into three and was an apparatus for dropping seed into left and right furrows at the same time as into the one under you. We pulled seed from the bag and dropped it into the horn. With a rustling sound it dropped into the furrows like falling rain.

The Group called it "improved agriculture." Compared to the Manchurian method it certainly was more efficient. But people who had lost their own lands and had come to Manchuria in labor mobilization squads, people working as coolies—they could only afford to scrupulously plant the little bit of seed they'd been given on a little plot of land. They couldn't even dream of using "improved agriculture." Group members scorned this "traditional method" of theirs. But I wondered how our "throw-away method" looked in the eyes of people who didn't dare neglect a single grain. Neither Sensei nor I could hold down feeling a bad conscience about them.

Though we lived in the corner of a remote great plain about three hours by train to the southwest of Mukden, and about two hours by wagon from the Daian prefecture office, thanks to Imperial Japan we pioneers could at least live without discomfort. Right after we arrived we were given horses and hogs. And though it was dry-field rice, we also were given rice. There were lavish rations of sorghum, sugar, soybean oil, tobacco, and salted salmon. Before long the Group also would have to join the forced supply system, they told us at the office, but for the moment there wasn't any need to worry about it. Garden crops like tomatoes, cucumbers, eggplants and watermelons ripened nicely. We planted potatoes and sowed cotton. Although it was late for sowing, the hours of sunlight were long enough that things would grow well in half the days they'd need in our homeland.

Manchurian farmers came to the Group from time to time to buy potatoes. Because the supply system was so strict, I was told that they would buy potatoes the Group had grown and deliver them to the authorities. And we wondered about that long line of people always around; it was Manchurian women waiting to get their trifling ration of cotton. I remember an indescribable resentment whenever I heard about Group members who went around selling their rations of tobacco and soap on the black market.

In the long sunshine of summer, weeding the sorghum fields really was a bitter chore. The heat was so fierce you couldn't compare it to the homeland. The rows were fantastically long, and when we'd finished a row we would have gone so far that our voices wouldn't carry back to the other end. If one person managed to weed two rows in a half day it was a good job. The only place to escape the sun was under the large willows which had been planted here and there as windbreaks. No matter how heated we were, even if we got dizzy, if we just went under the shade of these trees for a moment there'd again be a cooling breeze of a sort we never could savor in the homeland. And here in the evening as our sweat began to evaporate, a full-red sun would sink into the far wide horizon. We were always caught by this amazing sight.

The sorghum grew and at last the tufted ears hung down. Where the horses had trampled the fields at planting time, a road had developed. But we were afraid that bandits might jump out as we went through fields so thick with sorghum, so even in the daytime we avoided walking alone.

We picked cotton, dug potatoes, and harvested soybeans. In preparation for the long winter we also reaped fodder for the horses. Radishes, Chinese cabbage, eggplant —everything had to be prepared in a way that would preserve it. Evenings and mornings grew surprisingly chilly, and we needed to use the *ondoru* [Manchurian- and Korean-style heater with pipes beneath the floor].

One day the leader came to see Sensei. He complained that the members weren't getting along. "They're resisting group labor; they are all being individualistic and thinking only about what is right in front of them. They want to do the 'wintering over' work on the fields, but if they don't work together it's useless. And yet nobody can agree on what to do; no matter how much we're scolded by the prefecture people, the members fuss about everything the staff suggests and nothing gets done."

The soil itself was fertile, but they had been operating for two years without fertilizer. To make a proper job of "wintering over" we'd have to speed up the weathering of the soil. Sensei listened silently, and that evening he called the male members together in the bachelors' dormitory. All our Shinkyō men went too. Women and children stayed home and went to bed early. Much much later one of our young men rushed in and shook us awake. "Sensei wants you—everybody come quick."

Once we got to the meeting, we could sense the taut atmosphere. The members were seated in a circle around Sensei, and nobody was saying much. When he saw that we had come in quietly and sat down together, Sensei softly began to speak.

"We're at the point where the Development Group has to sink or swim. We Shinkyō people came here with the intention of burying our bones in this land. If this Group collapses we still won't go back to the homeland, so I mean to carry through now even if it kills me. Those who are willing to die with me, come along. Those who don't like it, I want you to go back to the homeland tomorrow.

"And now to show that I'm determined to do it, I'm going to sign here in blood. The Shinkyō people who want to come with me can sign in blood after me."

He put his left thumb into his mouth and bit into it. With the blood that oozed out, he quietly pressed a blood-seal under his name. We will absolutely follow Sensei in anything. It is not the blind subservience of a slave; it is because we're sure that if we follow him we will not be mistaken, and because our experience so far has proved it. Without a word we followed him in order of age, each cutting a finger with a knife and signing in blood. The women and I too; each of us cut her little finger with the knife. Even the grade-school children did it. I was in tears.

Sensei said, "The other Group members too—I'd like those who are willing to struggle together through this crisis to sign in blood as we did." Moved by having seen even children signing in blood, the members battled to be first. Somebody said, "Is blood from chapped hands good enough?" and the atmosphere relaxed a little.

Sensei, who ordinarily doesn't speak in a command voice, was like a stranger as he gave orders to those around him. "I want the leader and all the staff to come here." Somebody leaped to his feet as though possessed, and he must have flown to the office to get them, because at once the leader, the manager, and the marshal raced in.

A tense silence—as though cold water had been thrown

on them—hung over the whole crowd. The staff looked overwhelmed. They were frightened by the sight of the signing in blood. The leader covered his face with his hands and squatted down. "Please, enough. Won't you stop doing that?"

"Mr. Leader, it is an expression of the members' determination. We would rather hear a word of encouragement from you," said Sensei. They continued until all hundred members had signed.

Released from the tension, everybody had a relaxed look on his face. At some point it had gotten light outside. Sensei said, "Well, now we start anew."

"In any case that's something to be glad about," said the leader. And the marshal added, "With this the Group has had a new birth."

"Thank you all," said the leader, "I'm truly grateful. I thought I wanted you to stop signing in blood, at least . . . but all right, it's already done. How about taking a short nap and then getting to work? All right, Sensei?"

"No, that's no good. At a time when we are all keyed up, we should do our 'wintering-over' right away. If you haven't the grit to carry on without sleep for one or two nights, you're not a development pioneer. How about it? I think we should go right out and set to work."

They all raised their hands and shouted agreement. Their eyes were sparkling. Their drowsiness already had been wiped away and they jumped up eagerly. The sun had begun to rise.

We lined up in front of the office. The rule was that members would perform morning honors every day. We were supposed to gather at the office, bow to the east, and go through morning ceremonies that began with *Yamato bataraki* ["patriotic exercises," i.e. calisthenics]. But lately attendance had been declining and amounted to not much more than the Shinkyō people and the rest of team one. This morning, however, the whole Group turned out.

The leader took charge. "Bow to the East! Silent prayer!" Then he called numbers for calisthenics. With fresh enthusiasm we stretched our arms, bent our legs, and put all our strength into doing patriotic exercises. At the end we gave three banzais. The leader stretched his arms wide and said, *"Sumera mikoto iyasaka"* [hurrah for the Emperor]. We responded with "iyasaka iyasaka iyasaka!"

> "We of the Development Group follow the great policies of our Imperial forefathers. We put our hearts together and offer our bodies to the sacred task of developing Manchuria. We vow to serve in accord with the Imperial Will. Sumera mikoto iyasaka!"

As soon as we finished breakfast the whole Group hurried out to the communal fields. I don't really know how many thousands of acres there were, but it was an immense tract. Tens of horses lined up drawing plows—to call it spectacular is no exaggeration.

The leader and the manager brought candy out to the fields as a treat. People were plowing as hard as they could, not even turning to look. I'd never seen such a show of collective effort. And the bothersome chores of "wintering-over" were finished off in a trifling amount of time.

Mr. O wasn't able to watch this amazing communal labor. He was off on a business trip. He found himself frequently away on Group affairs and was absent as often as not. The fact that the members had gotten together so effectively actually seemed to displease him. He appeared to be uneasy because the members had followed Sensei. Mr. O's antipathy for Sensei was turned against the leader too. Where Shinkyō's affairs were at stake, Mr. O began to oppose the leader every time. The agricultural advisor, on the other hand, grew fond of us: he said we had the ability to understand and we were diligent in our farming. And so Mr. O took a disliking to *him*, and it grew more and more difficult for him to stay in the Group.

Soon the leader took ill and died. We thought that one

cause of it was the trouble he'd had because of us, and we were deeply sorry about that. The agricultural advisor had earlier moved away to a development group in Northern Manchuria; he wasn't able to stand Mr. O's pressures. And I was afraid that if the situation didn't change, the Group's future would be gloomy.

CHAPTER NINE
The end of a lost war

Sensei and I returned to Kasama in January, 1945, in order to lead the remaining Shinkyō members from there to Manchuria. Only eight of us were left in Kasama, women and old folk who had stayed to take care of our paddies under Mitani's direction. Forty-seven others had emigrated in 1943 and 1944.

Perhaps because Sensei overworked himself, he had to have an appendectomy and just did not recover speedily. So the final migration had to be put off and put off; and then seven families of acquaintances who were being evacuated from bombed-out Osaka came to stay with us. Our family rooms, which had been silent for some time, grew a little noisy. Each of the evacuee families was in business in Osaka, so the husbands stayed there. We gave each family a room of its own.

When we took them in, Sensei told them, "Since we eat together at Shinkyō, I think it would make for better feelings and be more economical if you all would cook with us and eat the same food while you're under the same roof." But they didn't listen; they trusted their money to get them food on the black market, and every day they had luxurious meals of a kind we could not afford. We were eating wheat, they were eating rice.

We let them freely take charcoal, firewood, vegetables —anything we grew or made at Shinkyō—and since we never once watched them, we had no idea who took what or how much. Of course they handed over money for it to one of the Shinkyō women when it was convenient and at what they figured was a suitable price, but we had no guarantee as to whether or not we got fair value. We didn't touch any of the money they gave us: we put it all into a savings-box for national defense donations. We were convinced that this did not amount to black marketeering. So we were puzzled by what happened on August 3rd, right before the end of the war.

We had just finished breakfast and were relaxing for a moment when seven or eight police from the Sakurai station crowded in on us, their faces full of anger. As we started to get up, they commanded us, "Stay there! Don't make a move!" Four of them stood by the bench to block our way, and said domineeringly, "Don't any of you say a word to each other!" Even so, I poured tea and offered them some.

The others made Mitani lead them, and apparently went to search the storerooms and family rooms. What were they looking for anyway? We could only watch. Sensei and Yamanaka were staring vacantly. Before long the searchers were done. The one they called Sergeant said, "Ozaki, that woman, and Yamanaka—I want the three of you to get in the wagon and come to headquarters."

They made the three of us sit on mats in the exercise room on the second floor of the station. Each of us had to face a different wall so we couldn't look at each other. A patrolman was swinging a bamboo sword and slamming it against a board, apparently to make us afraid. After a while we were led into separate rooms, and the interrogations began.

Even then I was not sure what I was suspected of, though I did think of one thing. It happened the day before, when we heard that an American carrier-based plane had crashed on a peak near the village, and everybody went to see. A huge pine had been toppled, the nose of the plane had crashed through its branches and was stuck into the ground. The pilot had been killed outright, and was lying on his back as though asleep. His forehead was smashed, and a darkish bloodstain had left a huge mark. The villagers were milling around the corpse and one or two were shouting, "Beast! Serves you right!" and kicking his head and legs. Without thinking, I blurted out, "The poor guy!" and bowed in silent prayer. Sensei said, "When you are dead, you are the same as a god. This one didn't come to attack Japan because he wanted to; it was his country's orders." He had died with a photo of a young woman—his wife or girlfriend—in his breast pocket.

When I happened to look ahead about four or five meters, I saw several police squatting in a circle talking something over. It startled me. Maybe they'd overheard what Sensei and I had said. We had been told of people who had been thrown in the pigpen [jail] for saying something stupid. An uneasy shudder went through me, but I had since forgotten about it.

I was asked the usual questions about name, date of birth, years of school. Then the policeman asked me gravely, "Don't you remember what you did wrong?"

"There isn't anything I can think of. So you tell me, please."

He glanced at my face and said, "All right, if you don't remember anything, that's that. I'll put you in the pigpen and have you think about it a while."

As he said it, he signalled to a patrolman with his chin. I wasn't given a chance to speak; the officer made me walk. When I heard the steel door clank behind me I knew that this was the pigpen. I found myself turned loose into a dark, cold cell. I walked to all corners of the dark interior. Three sides had fairly thick walls; when I hit them with clenched fists, they gave off a dull sound. My foot stubbed on something, and when I groped with my hands I found it was a wooden chamber-pot. After a while my eyes began to get accustomed to the dark and a very unpleasant stench came to me; I could see a little more clearly that the walls were smeared with excrement and covered with scribblings.

"Sergeant——keeps you long."

"When I get out I'll kill Judge ——"

Along with them were months and days that had been marked off. The place was full of letters and marks I had a hard time deciphering.

What had happened to Sensei and Yamanaka? I knew my nerves were getting sharp like the points of needles. I was all ears. I was quite sure all the voices were talking about Sensei, and I couldn't stand it. I could hear them saying, "Send that one to the military police," and I could hear them saying, "It is a felony." And yet there was nothing I could do. The time went slowly.

Soon I thought I heard a high voice speaking angrily. The door opened, a woman was shoved in, and she collapsed in front of my legs. The door shut with a clank. She stared at one spot for a while, not saying anything. It was dark, so maybe she couldn't see me. In a while she raised her voice and began crying. "What were you put in here for?" I asked, but without answering she pressed her breasts with both hands and cried loudly. Was she a little crazy? I tried again. When she finally seemed to get what I said, she suddenly put her hands together.

"I did something truly unforgivable. I stole pumpkins from somebody else's garden. As I was running away I dropped my ration book so they knew who did it. Please forgive me."

"Oh well, you don't have to make apologies to me. I'm somebody who's been put in here the same as you."

"You mean you stole something too?"

"I don't remember stealing anything."

"Well, if that's the case, what did you do wrong?"

"I don't know what I did wrong; I'm trying to think what it might be."

In a little while another woman was put in. She seemed to be a mere girl. She said she had been caught at the train station as she was taking some rice she'd saved from her own meals and going to her uncle's place. "As I was being put in here I saw uncle being put into the next cell, so I suppose it means I will have to tell the truth."

"It's best for people to tell the truth," I said.

The three of us rubbed sleeves and talked together through the night. Next day the two of them were called out and did not come back. I guessed they had been excused.

Some days passed. I was taken out. I thought the air inside the station was amazingly fresh, and I drew great breaths of it to my heart's content. My eyes were dazzled. I don't know how I was taken where, but I was made to sit in front of an officer who held some red-line stationery marked District Attorney's Office.

Name, date of birth, years of schooling, the same questions as before. "Why is it that you people have to have some sort of communal life?"

I didn't answer.

"The other day when we searched the house, I saw it. Why do you have to put things like your clothes all together?"

"Our communal life isn't one that anybody especially planned, it just worked out that way."

"Now what is that supposed to mean?"

"At the beginning we were simply faithful believers in Tenri; but when we heard from Ozaki Sensei, who was a missionary, that making idols the object of faith was a device for stealing money and goods from believers, and that because he hated such beggaring he had smashed his altar and was going to follow a faith that truly would help people, we agreed with him and took down the altar of the village chapel. But that caused bad blood between Sensei and

113

the village bosses, and the upshot was that Sensei and the four families who followed him were ostracized from the village. We had no choice but to take up collective production, but if it is only work that you do together, all sorts of difficulties come up. While we were wrestling with those difficulties one by one, we happened to end up in 'communal living.' "

"Hm. Well, that's enough on that. However, you didn't have to go as far as to pool your kimonos, did you?"

"We kept our clothes separate at first. But if A wants to buy something he needs, and you are working collectively, he is likely to feel constrained because of B. And B on his part is likely to feel he wants one even if he doesn't need it, as long as A's going to buy one. And this causes much waste. But if you pool your clothing, you can put idle pieces to use; every year we were able to turn our clothing-ration coupons back to the village office. We got a certificate of merit from them for it. If everybody in Japan thought this way just about clothes, they would be able to squeeze out a lot more money for the sake of the war, wouldn't they?"

He seemed to back off just a little. "Hm. Okay. Next, why is it your group is called *Shinkyō Dōjin* [people of the same state of mind]?"

"That doesn't have any deep meaning either. When the four families came together, they brought things that had each family's name on them—things like paper lanterns and parasols. These were worn out in a year or two. And when we ordered new ones we wondered about what name to have put on them. We even talked about taking the first letter of each family's name. Some time earlier we had given some savings to the township office as a national defense donation. They sent word that we should give them the name of the donor, but Sensei said, 'If you have to have a donor's name, how about writing everybody's name? Or if that is too much trouble, we will just forget about donating.

Or maybe we should put down a fake name? Why not make it, "The group of the same state of mind"?'

"Later when we had forgotten about it, something unexpected came by mail in a huge envelope. It had *Mainichi Newspaper Corporation* on it, and *Shinkyō Dōjin* on the front; inside there was a certificate of thanks for the donation. It was a good hint, so after that we began to write and talk of ourselves sometimes as Shinkyō and sometimes as Dōjin. In short, it really came about by accident."

The officer hadn't written anything after putting down my name, date of birth, etc.; he just listened. But his expression was grave, asking why? why? and not offering a trace of sympathy or indulgence. I chose each word carefully, trying to confess honestly.

"I noticed when we searched the house that you get good crops. Are you buying chemical fertilizer on the black market?"

What on earth was this bureaucrat trying to get out of me? I don't know about other families, but in those days we couldn't even hope to buy on the black market. I suspected that somebody in the village had made false charges.

"I don't know much about farming, but Sensei's always saying, 'Better to enrich the land than put chemicals on it.' All of us get up at four a.m. and go cut grass from the hills. Then we collect barnyard manure and make a ripe compost. Even when we piss or when we spit, we never wastefully throw away *anything* that can go into compost. We've been diligently enriching the soil for a decade."

"Oh, all right. The last thing I want to ask is why you all call your leader Ozaki *Sensei*. What is the reason for that?"

"He used to be a missionary, and so we began calling him Sensei. It's not for this or that reason in particular, it's just a custom. He says himself that he doesn't like it, that it is not appropriate to call him Sensei any more—that it might be different if he was a scholar or a sage, but after all he is just a broken-down priest."

"What kind of relation do you and he have?"

I didn't answer.

"I cannot understand you if you are silent. The relationship is a physical one, isn't it?"

"I hear that people refer to Sensei's and my association as one of 'red dogs in heat.' No matter what they say about me, I cannot leave him."

"Oh, all right. That's enough for today."

I was sent back again to the dark jail. Some days passed, but I could not get any news of Ozaki Sensei. Then a big tall Korean woman was put in for brewing bootleg sake. She clung to the lattice over the door, shouting Mercy! Mercy! Eventually when she had attracted the attention of the guard, she handed him some money and said, "Sensei, please go buy me some medicine." He was back soon and shoved it through the slot, saying "That's two days' dose, now." Still crying Mercy! Mercy!, she swallowed the whole dose at one gulp. I watched quietly, and soon the woman seemed to settle down and said, "You did something wrong?"

Shaking my head, I said "What have I done? Even I don't know."

"Stupid!" she said. "Get help!"

"Get help? Who from?"

"From the police, that's who."

"How do you do that?"

"You have parents? Brothers and sisters? A husband? Have them get help."

"Where do they go?"

"Fool! Don't you know anything? They should go ask for help at a policeman's house. They take money and food there."

If what she said was true, I had to laugh at my own ignorance of the world. But could it really work?

"You Japanese are hopeless. Why should they put away a weakling like you? We Koreans stick together. At times like this we all take things to a policeman's house and bribe him to help. Japanese are so greedy."

I began to think she might be right. If it could be done smoothly, I'd be excused and Sensei could be saved. I was trying to plan it.

"When I get out, I'll go to your house and tell them to get up a campaign for you," she said.

"What's your name?"

"Toyama."

"Toyama? How do you spell it?"

"You know how to write?"

There was a rattle as the door opened, and through the slot the guard shoved in a bamboo-wrapped lunch somebody had sent her. He also put in the usual jail food for me. I hadn't eaten it once since I had come. It was in a wooden box twenty centimeters long, ten wide and five deep, and was nothing but soybeans with a thin mix of wheat grains. One corner held two slices of very vinegary cucumber pickles cut so thin it impressed me. The first day, I gave it back to the guard without touching it. He warned me, "If you don't eat it, tomorrow you won't get anything." But I just could not get it down my throat.

However, all the women who were thrown into that pigpen with me were kind to me; and since they shared their lunches with me, I got along without the jail food. Those women were being questioned about things like theft, bootleg sake, or ration crimes; they got their lunches from home and in one or two days they were sent away. I was the only one always left.

The Korean woman took a big rice-ball from its wrapper and offered it to me, and she gave me two big slices

117

of pickled radish. They were hot, with a lot of red pepper, but delicious. "Koreans are pros at making pickles," she boasted. I was glad to hear from her about how they wash and spice things for pickling.

Next day she was called out and did not come back. I passed several days alone, then was called out again for a third interrogation. It looked as though I had been led before the Chief himself. He spoke with unexpected courtesy.

"Ahem. In communal living are there things like common-law rules?"

"What would that be? Could you please give me an example?"

"For example, at meals you must eat up everything that's been cooked—rules like that."

When I heard that, the idea hit me—the onlookers. I could see the faces of the evacuees; they were the ones who had turned on us. In the beginning the seven evacuee families had bought black market food and had eaten luxuriously; eventually they were down to harvesting weeds and eating bran. Sensei said to them, "Since we don't know how long this war may last, how would it be if you all ate with the farmers?" But they said they couldn't take our wheat diet and did not want to cook together with us. Until then any one of them who had given us a hand at work had been invited to eat with us, but now we decided to hold a group dinner for all of them and us several times a month. The Shinkyō people would not eat any of it; we would leave it all for them. But they not only ate their fill, they carried food away with them. Sensei is full of sympathy but he is also very fastidious, and he was disgusted by their gluttony.

"When we eat together, it is all right to fill yourselves as full as you want, but who said anything about taking it home with you? Eat it here before you leave."

I remembered this and described it in detail. The examiner seemed to understand it all right. "What is your relationship with this man Ozaki?"

"When I was young I went to Ozaki to be saved. And although I had been living with complete faith, my faith was upset by the unexpected illness of Ozaki's child. After I struggled with myself for a long time, I realized that my faith was in error. People talk about 'self-salvation' and 'salvation by others,' but in either case, I thought, 'supplication' is not the essence of religion; and with that I felt I had had a great awakening [*satori*]. Soon afterwards I couldn't bear to live anymore, and I resolved to take Sensei's beloved child with me in death."

The Chief interrupted me, "Just a moment, please. You just said you had a great awakening, but why does somebody who has had an awakening want to die? What kind of *state of mind* is that?" He emphasized the phrase.

"I had thought it through and realized that although a person can keep on living, no matter how painful things are, as long as he wants to do something or be somebody, my trouble was I didn't care. So it was all right with me if I lived and all right if I died. And in any case, I thought, if I die I might as well take with me one of the seeds of Sensei's sorrow, as a way of repaying his kindness. In short, I thought I'd kill myself and take his crippled child with me. When he realized that, Sensei washed his hands of the missionary life. Now that I mention it, that was one of our starting points—our communal life centers on a condition of faith and spiritual peace."

As I said this, the face of one of the evacuee wives bobbed into my mind. When she was younger, she had been distressed by her husband's wild living, had clung to Sensei and taken his advice, and somehow had pulled through. And I definitely thought she had an affection for Sensei that went beyond the ordinary bounds of faith. At least when her eyes fell on Sensei it was obviously a look that was aware of the opposite sex. So I guessed she was jealous of me and had informed on me; otherwise the police wouldn't have any reason to go into my private life.

"Did you sell rice to the evacuees on the black market?"

"Yes."

"How much did you sell, and what was the price?"

"That I don't know."

I answered right off, but it was the first time I realized that I had been hauled in for a ration offense. Stupid, yes, I really was stupid; but I hadn't thought of it until then.

We had felt uneasy about that woman who begged us for rice—she seemed to think that if she would just offer cash, then obviously we would share with her the rice we were growing for ourselves.

One time when she was over at our place as usual, Sensei couldn't resist telling her, "You seem to feel it is all right to buy our private rice with your cash; but if we lose the war, that money will be no more than just paper."

I chipped in, "You realize, don't you, that we are making do with only five shaku of rice per meal? Also, the Japanese in Manchuria are short on rice, but even so to provide for emergencies each of them puts aside a cup apiece every time the ration is distributed."

She colored a little and hurried out with a parting shot. She warned us that since the seller of black market rice is punished but the buyer isn't, if we were going to act this way she was ready for it. Sure enough, the next day several plain clothesmen turned up, called the evacuees one by one to the corner of our dining room, and interrogated them. Three or four days later we were taken to headquarters.

The Chief asked nothing more and I had to return to my cell again. After that it was as though my existence had been completely forgotten; I wasn't ever called. To a person who has been jailed, thirty minutes or an hour of questioning actually is a pleasure. At the very least, during that time you can breathe the outside air. The cell is so dark that even if your fingers crush one of the insects crawling over your body, you can't tell if it is a louse or a flea. It is damp, and the stench coming from the chamber pot is unbearable. The longer he is jailed, the more a suspect grows weary waiting for his interrogation.

I'm not sure how many days passed after that, but one day—it was a hot day—the guard came and peered through the bars of each cell and shouted, "Everybody stand! Stand up! Can't you stand?"

"Okay? Everybody listen closely. You are criminals but you are also Japanese, so now we are going to let you hear the Emperor's voice too. Come out quietly."

The steel doors opened, and the faces of the suspects, grimy with dust and sweat, followed the guard as he led them out. About thirty of them altogether, all men except me. They made us stand erect without moving, in front of a radio. They said it was the Emperor's voice, but there was so much static that before I could figure out what he was talking about, the Imperial Broadcast was over. Having come outside for the first time in quite a while, I was so wobbly, so dazed, the stimuli were so strong, that I guess I didn't have much energy left over for paying attention to the radio. It was the following day, when a kindly guard informed us that Japan had lost the war and he didn't know if we would be excused, that I finally realized that the Emperor's voice had announced the end of the war.

The third day after that, the prison showed no signs of life. I thought I heard the voice of the Sensei I was longing for, and I became all ears. Somebody was saying, "Sharpy is away today, so I want you to stay here until tomorrow."

"All right. Is Mrs. Sugihara here?" No doubt about it, it was Sensei. The voices came closer. There was the sound of a door clanking open. "Ah! Here!" said Sensei, and I hurried to get up and see him in the dark.

He looked a little thin, but his eyes were shining with life. He seemed more healthy than I had expected. Apparently he was put in the innermost cell. That night I waited for the jail to quiet down in sleep and then tried to call him. I put my mouth against the grill.

"Sensei. Sensei. Are you all right?"

"I'm all right. How about you?"

"Me too." I lowered my voice a little. "Sensei, what have we been put in here for?"

"They suspect us of circulating false rumors, of being spies, of being communists. I guess there's more, but for any one of them you have to go to the penitentiary for ten years. If we hadn't lost the war, it would be a lifetime sentence."

So we were "traitors." Ask me what a "traitor" is and I couldn't even guess. It made me shiver just to hear the word. No wonder there hadn't been a full interrogation, that nothing could be sent in to me, that I had simply been put away.

"Circulating false rumors—what did we say?"

"I told the evacuee woman that if we lost the war her money would be just so much paper. It seems that if you mention losing the war, that is circulating false rumors."

"Then that means she informed on us, doesn't it?"

"Well, I don't know."

"Aren't you mad at her?"

"I'm not even thinking about it. Instead, I'm thinking that how when we get out of here, I want to take it easy as never before."

"That's for sure."

Our voices were as low as possible, but we had been overheard by the guard, and he shouted at us like thunder, "What the hell are you gabbing about? Quiet down and get to sleep. We put you in separate cells because you're not supposed to talk—don't you know that? Keep jabbering and you'll get nothing to eat tomorrow!"

Next day I could sense a stirring in the jail, and a handsome, rosy-cheeked young man was brought to Sensei's cell. Judging from what the guard said, he was being put in because he had a fight with somebody. Toward evening the guard whispered to him, "The other man died. But don't let it get you down."

That night I waited again for the jail to quiet down, and again tried to talk to Sensei. "What did he do?"

"This one . . . he killed a man by mistake. He was so broken up he couldn't eat his dinner, so I'm trying to console him now. You learn about life from everything. I was telling him I'm going to the penitentiary later on too, so he can go on ahead and wait there for me. We will be in prison together to start off on a new life. Anyway, what I said calmed him down and he resolved to take it all as the first step towards learning about life."

"Ah, that's good. But do you have to go to the penitentiary too?"

"It seems that way."

"But 'thought crimes' were cancelled when the war was lost, isn't that true?"

"That's true, but because I sold rice to the evacuee, it looks as though I'll have to spend ten years in prison."

"How much rice do you suppose you sold her?"

"A few bushels; whatever the police say."

"But that's terrible! You can't remember, and so everything depends on what they say!"

"That's that, we can't do anything about it. But in any case I mean to go to the penitentiary with this young man. We're going to study an unknown society. You know, I like being a farmer, and I'm thinking that before I go to prison, I wish I could see how Shinkyō's rice has grown. It's already well into September, so it must have grown high. If they will let me do farm work in the penitentiary too, I won't complain."

"I'm going with you."

"No, you'll be released."

Why just him? I put my energy into the argument.

After all, Sensei had not sold rice that was his personally; it belonged to all of Shinkyō. If anybody had to go to prison, then all the members should go, and not just Sensei.

"You all have to keep up the farm, so it is better for me to take the blame myself. You keep yourselves healthy until I come back."

Endless tears streamed down my cheeks. I sobbed curses at that evacuee. What a crook!

Sensei said, "She thought only the seller would get punished, so she told the police that plenty of bushels were involved. Then she learned that the buyer also can be punished and now she is apparently trying to trim down the amount. Whatever the amount was, since I don't remember, I say it was exactly what the police tell me."

Having lived a month inside that dark cell, tortured by mosquitoes at night and by lice and fleas in the daytime, I was terribly short on sleep, had not eaten well, and was very wobbly whenever I stood up. The dog days were over, and in the waning heat of September the mornings and evenings were chilly. They allowed a blanket to be sent in to me. Outdoors in the autumn sunshine it looked beautifully clear. A dim shaft of sunlight about five inches square came straight down from the high vent window. I put out my hands and feet and tried to get some sun on my pale, dried-up skin.

One day a creepy feeling, bubbling like soapsuds, welled up in my chest. Suddenly I retched. Red blood flew from my mouth. I quickly grabbed some paper, and as I retched I coughed two or three times. Fresh blood flowed out constantly. I forced my heart to keep calm, closed my eyes and laid down. Each time I took a breath there was a bubbling sound somewhere in my chest. When I retched, it was blood. I had heard that salt water is best when you have to stop the bleeding quickly. I stood up and called Sensei. I tried to shout but I wondered if I had made any sound after all. However, he seemed to hear me.

Sensei and everybody in the jail put their voices together and called the guard for me. They were a great help.
The guard came all right, but when I asked if there was any
salt water, he ignored me. How heartless can you get? "Tomorrow when Sharpy comes, tell him you are sick and get
him to send you out of here," he said, and went away.

The official was flustered by my plight. Next morning
I was given a temporary release. I went back to Shinkyō
and went to bed. Of course I had to keep absolutely still.
But while I was in bed, I worried so about Sensei that I
couldn't bear it. We had been able to talk together, but I
had had to part from him without seeing him. Maybe in one
sense life in jail was better than this; it offered the security
of being near him. I hadn't realized that Shinkyō without
Sensei could be so empty.

It turned out that that evacuee woman had gotten completely high-handed. She said what she felt like, right to
our people's faces—that they should give her some land
because she wanted to farm it, that they should give her
rice so she could have Sensei's crime reduced, and so on.
I was told that among her relatives was a man who had influence with the police; he was a boss in his district, and
even if you were caught with ration goods the police would
close the case without reporting it if you appealed to them
through him. Later it turned out that in our case the information to the police had gone via this man.

Anyway, a short time later somebody hurried in and
told us that Sensei had been sent to the city hospital. It was
good news that he was out of jail, but hearing he was hos-
pitalized set other worries to brewing. Because it had come
not many days after his appendix operation, his long stay
in the pigpen probably had been too much for him; he had
a hernia and was in sharp pain. Not being allowed out of
bed, all I could do was fret about it. But in the end the
charges against him all were dropped.

Sensei's return home was a jolt to the evacuees, to put

it mildly. They had expected he would be put away and wouldn't come back for a long time. Right there in front of him, without even being asked about it, they all began to talk about the affair, and started to argue. So-and-so had been the first to squeal; so-and-so had fooled us and snitched some of our goods; you could order him to pay but he didn't have the money any more. Soon they couldn't stand being with us any more, I guess; and they went away in ones and twos.

During my twenty-five days in jail I had chased a happy dream, and consoled myself with it. Every time I was interrogated, I was asked about my relationship with Sensei. How should I explain it? I didn't know what to say, and when I got out I definitely wanted to arrange it so I could use without fear the words "husband and wife." But when I left jail, the dream died away.

At the end of 1945, some officers came from prefectural police headquarters, took photos of all of Shinkyō, and asked us about our methods of operation. Oh no, here they go again, I thought as I watched them, but they told us, "Well, from now on you are back in the world again, so put your minds at ease about it." Next somebody from the Public Affairs Section of the Occupation Forces came riding up in a jeep and inquired in detail about our being jailed and how the police treated us. And then—sure enough, we thought—some men came from the Communist Party.

They told us, "Since this place already has taken the form of a full communism, if you will join the Party, your ideals will be realized both in name and in fact. You really should join us."

I thought it would be rude to refuse them bluntly, so I tried to say something that would console them a little. "I suppose people in the Communist Party are convinced that what they are doing is right. But the public looks at you coldly, doesn't it? On that score it is the same with us. So we understand very well how you feel, and we will be glad to have you drop in and visit us from time to time."

Another time a young man came around canvassing for the Party as he sold patent medicines door to door, and we invited him to spend the night with us. Sensei listened to his enthusiastic talk about the Party, then asked him, "In your Party do the top people live the same kind of life you do?"

"Of course not," said the young man. But he wasn't able to convince Sensei, who pierced every reason given to explain the difference, and in the end the young man fell silent. Next morning he left, saying, "I'm leaving the Party and going home. After talking to you last night, I began to feel that I wanted to go home. When I realized how Mother and Father must be worrying about me, I wanted to go home as soon as I could."

An American missionary also came. He looked carefully at how we live, and was so touched he said, "The spirit of this life is the very heart of Christ. This is true religion." Then the American MPs came. It was some sort of attitude survey, but they also told us, "This is democracy through and through." One after another, people with different viewpoints and occupations came to Shinkyō. Some went away happy and some downcast. Life was in turmoil in those postwar days. What had changed was the outside world; our feelings had not changed at all.

CHAPTER TEN
We return and rebuild

As the third team delayed its move to Manchuria, Japan's defeat hit like Mukden lightning. It not only forced us to change our plans, it cut off all contact with our group over there. There was nothing we could do but just earnestly hope they were healthy and safe. The topic inevitably came up every time I talked to Sensei. As we checked the radio and newspapers, or talked with repatriates, we grew more and more worried.

Suddenly and without any notice, our group returned. It was May of 1946. In the eight months since the war's end eight of them had died of malnutrition, and the rest were a sad sight as they got off the train at Haibara. An old man from a hardware store in town gave each of them a piece of bread, explaining that it was the death-day anniversary of his son, and that he was doing it as a memorial offering. They certainly looked enough like beggars to give one a feeling of compassion. (As a way of saying thanks, that winter when we had made our charcoal we delivered some to the old man to use in lighting his first fire of the season. We heard later that he was so moved by it he gave a sermon in front of the station, saying "humanity has not yet fallen to the ground.") I went out to meet them on the way, but even though we had parted only the year before, their looks had changed so much and they all had gotten so thin I hardly could tell who was who. When they said to me, "Please realize that the faces you don't see here belong to those who died," I looked at them one after another, but it wasn't easy to decide who was missing. One boy—he should have been in fifth grade by then—must have desperately forced his starved body to hold out until he could tread the soil of the old home village. As he came to the entry of the communal kitchen, he suddenly fell over; and there he died.

They had no food or clothing; all they brought back was their bodies. And there was no reason to expect us to have anything to spare. So it left us no choice but to plan a new start.

At the time we began collective operations in 1938, we had 19.6 acres of paddy. But in swapping fields to get our land together where it is now, we had had to sacrifice seven acres. Then in order to migrate we let out five acres to tenants, and because of the newly-issued farmland laws these would never be returned to us. So all we had left was seven acres. With so little paddy you couldn't expect all of us to make a living by farming—and we soon had seven more families.

Seven or eight people from Kagawa—they had been living with us in Manchuria—paid a call at Shinkyō at New Year's time, 1947. Through this contact seven families (some twenty people) joined us. Each of them came for their own particular reasons. One man had been doing very well in business until he went to Manchuria; but when he came home penniless he found the atmosphere in his home village cool, and he was obliged to become a black marketeer. Another was still doing all right running an orchard, but somehow he found he had lost interest in it. Still another had had to leave his wife and parents in Manchuria when he repatriated, and the wounds in his heart simply would not heal. And so on, every one of them different.

All together we were thirteen families, a crowd of more than sixty people. Surely, dividing seven acres of paddy and 2½ of unirrigated fields equally among that many families was pointless. If we did that, all of us would be in such straits we probably could not even afford to drink water.

["Water drinker" is an old Japanese idiom for a person so poor he cannot even afford tea.] It was possible to get back the tenant paddy by pleading special circumstances with the prefectural agricultural bureau; but Ozaki Sensei, cooperating with the aims of the new land law, withdrew the petition.

So we sowed cotton on our unirrigated fields. Then we spun it and wove cloth, and made work clothes and nemaki.

We raised sheep and wove homespun.

We raised goats and got milk.

We raised hogs as our source of protein.

We grew sugar-cane and got sugar.

We grew sweet potatoes, and every night until midnight we made candy from them. We sold it in Osaka.

We planted rape-seed for the second crop in the paddy. We intended to press oil from it only for our own consumption, but we had to take out a license for the oil-press anyway. So instead it became one of the enterprises which secured our future.

Since we couldn't afford to buy chemical fertilizer on the black market, we got up every morning at two and went to Haibara to collect nightsoil; on the way back we also picked up garbage. When we came home we went out to cut weeds from the hills. Then we mixed weeds and animal manure with the garbage and nightsoil to make a compost. All of these were young men's chores, but Sensei joined in from time to time.

We got our nightsoil from the Haibara Girls' School. And although the young men felt awkward even about going in and out of the school gates hauling a cart under the girls' chill glances, still, once they had dipped out the nightsoil they had to clean up the toilet neatly before they came back. It really must have been bitter for them. (One time the principal came out to Shinkyō, and he mentioned that the young men's conduct was good teaching material and was being praised at the school.) When they finished gathering the nightsoil, they would go get the sawdust we used for our daily fuel. They would tie the ox in front of the sawmill and without taking a break would go immediately to load sawdust on the cart. As soon as it was loaded, they would set off again for home. They got no relief from their chores even on rainy or windy days. And they scarcely ever loafed on the job. In town they were held up as model youth.

We couldn't care how it looked, we simply had to do it to survive. Old and young, male and female, there were no exceptions. We believe that the convictions you develop while laboring are the ones that create genuine human beings.

This kind of life continued for quite a long time. Our anger and antipathy about the ostracism already had grown pretty feeble. But that does not mean that an invisible sense of opposition and battle of wills with the villagers had disappeared. On the surface, neither we nor the villagers had discarded the cold-shoulder treatment. Of course, if we met them individually, we sometimes talked with real friendliness, but if there was a cluster of three or five of them and us, both sides looked the other way. You have to admit it was ridiculous for some people to be taking this attitude without questioning it since they had no idea of the reasons behind it. But perhaps a village, or village life, is basically like that.

The saying is that "evil runs a thousand miles," and the Shinkyō ostracism came to be known in distant places. In the village itself, it was a good thing there was some affability towards us on the part of a few. They helped by trading fields with us, and they kept us informed of the backbiting talk in the village. But this was done strictly in private. There was only one man who fairly openly expressed good will towards Shinkyō, and his name was Nomura.

The Seki gang's treatment of us was gradually coming under criticism; and in any case you cannot deny that the loss of the war, and the chain of events that followed it—

land reform and democratization—dealt a great blow to the gang's sphere of influence. So the idea that village offices always would be monopolized by one party and one faction was slowly crumbling away. Then came the first election for land-reform committeemen. Nomura had a different point of view than the Seki followers, so Ozaki Sensei backed his campaign and helped him get elected. A corner of the village power structure clearly had been broken down.

Next came the issue of the power line.

In order to press oil from our rape-seed, we naturally had to have a press, and to run the press we had to have a power line. However, since one hadn't yet been strung to the village, we not only had to buy a press, we had to pay to have a power line brought out. Once we brought out the line, the engines that had been in use until then wouldn't be needed of course; all the hullers and polishers and such could be run by electric motors. So Sensei said that as long as we were bringing the line to Shinkyō we might as well have it extended as far as the village co-op, and we had it done at our expense. Having been ostracized, we wouldn't have needed to be concerned about the village or its future development, but Sensei isn't that kind of man. However, the villagers not only were not pleased, they even complained about it, saying, "Because they were kicked out, they are doing this to show us up." We were indignant about the way they were rejecting our good will, but Sensei said with a calm voice, "It is thanks to the ostracism that we are able to live communally, isn't it?"

Sensei talked with Nomura about developing the village. At that time in 1947 all sorts of goods were still in short supply, fish especially. We almost never got any to eat in an inter-mountain village like Kasama. So Sensei hit on the idea of contracting to make fishnets for a Wakayama fishing cooperative. They could no longer get hemp from Manila, and were said to be using nets woven from straw. We could make those nets. But since it was necessary to learn the technique first, one of the villagers was given money to go to Wakayama.

They had agreed to pay for the nets with fish, and before we had even sent them any nets we got fish from them two or three times. The whole village eagerly shared them. However, it was going to be quite a while before we would be able to make nets. So for the time being, as compensation for the fish, we decided to make packaging ropes. But since everybody braided them differently, the ropes we made were not of the same standards, and the Wakayama people had difficulty using them. So Sensei consulted with Nomura and suggested that we make the ropes by village-wide collective labor. Through Nomura's urging we had all the ropemakers in the village assemble in our Obatake house. The idea of collective labor was passed without opposition, but the problem was what to do for a community workshop. There just wouldn't be enough time to go out now and cut trees from the hills, have them made into lumber, and put up a new building. However, luckily or unluckily the village shrine office was tilting and so badly rotted we never knew when it might fall over, so rather than rebuild it now, why not for the time being take it down from the shrine mound and use it as a workshop? This was Sensei's proposal. But the villagers all fell dumb.

"You are all thinking it would be an insult to the gods. But if it is for the betterment of their children, the guardian gods will be pleased, that's what I think. If we build a new shrine and give it back to them, they won't be angry. For the moment the ropemaking is what is urgent."

Everybody was as silent as before.

"Well, you all please think it over carefully." In order to give them time to think about it, Sensei came home. When maybe half an hour had passed, Sensei went back, but the house was silent. Nobody was there; only the cushions were left, still scattered across the floor where people had been sitting on them. When we saw that, Sensei and I unconsciously let out our breaths. It just went too much against common decency. For all of them to go home without a single goodbye, as though they were running away, was so ridiculous it went beyond just making us angry.

We had thought nobody was there, but Nomura was by himself, sitting with his head between his hands. When we asked what had happened, he made a sour face and said, "Ah, they said that the old business about smashing the gods had started again, and that if they went along with you and were caught off guard, who knows what might happen to them; that they had seen through it. So they all went home."

The next day five or six men—no, there may have been more, probably the village officers—came up with a cart full of milling and hulling machines, unloaded them in front of our Storehouse, and carried them into it without a word. The machines were ours. When the power line was brought in, we had donated them to the co-op workshop, explaining that we did not feel right about using them by ourselves and wanted the whole village to share them.

The village people had misinterpreted what we meant about the shrine office building; all they could think of was "gods you don't bother won't hurt you." That's why without saying anything about it, they had high-handedly come and returned the machinery. It depends on your point of view: could there be conduct so self-centered and spiteful? Sensei watched their childish bustling with a bitter smile. Even a noble man like Sensei couldn't help feeling like he had swallowed lead because of the way they were treating him in one matter after another.

But these painful experiences actually were fortunate for us. After that we decided to stop being burned by working for the good of the village. And so before we did anything else we would improve our own way of life. I don't believe that was selfish. The villagers would not change their ideas about us until they could see with their own eyes how our life was getting better. Therefore, even if we had to take a little detour, it would actually be better for the villagers in the long run. It was then that we hit on the idea of making use of the power line to start manufacturing tatami. We would use the straw from our rice and process it into mats. To do that we needed a mat-making machine, of course; without one we would get nowhere. But to buy one we needed 100,000 yen. And what could we do to get together 100,000 yen in cash? The agonizing struggle began: would we make this much money first or would all of us starve to death first? In other words, since the only asset we had that could be turned into ready cash was, after all, the rice we grew for ourselves, we kept ourselves alive by eating squash, and sold as much rice as we could on the black market.

In those days if you were a farm family and had even a little surplus of your own rice, you cheated the ration system and sold on the black market; and if you were a city family, you just couldn't exist on rationed foods alone and had to supplement them with blackmarket rice. So no matter how badly the government wanted to punish violations of the ration system it could not easily establish proof, and the sellers themselves did not have a very strong sense of guilt. Even so, for us to do it took great determination. We counselled ourselves that we had no reason to feel guilty, since we weren't selling rice in order to make profits or to get luxuries; we even were cutting down the amount of rice we actually needed to live on, so we could build up a sum in cash.

One day Yamanaka and Kin-chan [her son] wrapped bags of rice around their waists and went off to Osaka. They hid their swollen stomachs, Yamanaka with a mantle, Kin-chan with the winter overcoat he had worn back from Manchuria. Twice a day somebody would dress this way and travel to Osaka. Sometimes the women took turns at it. For the women it was a real strain, wrapping the rice in a furōshiki and concealing it in a shawl. Since it was an hour on foot to Haibara, an hour by train to Osaka, and another hour on foot to our destination there, the round trip covered six hours. Those who stayed behind would grow restless marking off the time. It would often happen that people were delayed for some reason or other, but still the feeling of waiting and worrying, now?, now?, was unbearable. Not only that, we had to live with it every day.

A winter day darkens so easily. As the sun sank and the time came for lights to go on in the village houses, we couldn't settle down. Waiting until the Yasuda people had finished work in the fields and gone home, I went out to the curve to greet our two coming back from Osaka. Sensei was saying something important; he was more worried than I was. He was fully determined that if they were caught in a police surveillance net he would go and shoulder the full blame. Not yet? Not yet? The wait lengthened. Sensei and I were going out and coming back in, standing and sitting impatiently.

"Have they any reason to get caught? The gods know our hearts are pure," somebody said to soothe us.

Another one tried to be brave. "It is different than bad stuff like robbing and killing. If you don't black-market, you can't go on eating, the way things are now."

A lot of them grumbled to themselves, "We're black-marketing to eke out the lives of more than sixty people. If it weren't for this, all we could do is die."

Anyway the chatter was distracting, since anything is better than waiting silently. Everybody was anxious to say something.

At last the figures of the two appeared in the distance. "They made it back!"

"Good. Good. Well, you are back safely again today without being caught. I was worried." Sensei was relieved.

One day six or seven of us went to the Matsuda tatami

Kitoé

shop at Kurozaki. Sensei asked the owner's wife if she would show us the workshop and the mat-making machinery. We had often come and sold straw to this shop—a twelve-mile round trip with a loaded cart on the steep road over Onna-yori Pass—and since they bought our straw at a relatively high price, we weren't completely unknown to them. But because we had come in a crowd and were asking to be shown the shop, the wife seemed to suspect something, and she did not look very pleased; however, she didn't refuse. A Korean father and son were there making tatami, and whenever they had a moment they were good enough to explain things to us. We took in their explanations with our hearts pounding, because we weren't just curious, we were imagining the day when we would be using the same kind of machine to make the same kind of mats. Then at that point the wife came in, reddened with anger and said to the Korean father, "Why are you showing that to them when you were told not to?" and slammed back out.

As he watched her leave, he said in a small voice, "Japanese got small heart. That why lose in war."

We knew that the machine was called a Futada Continuous. We bought our Futada Continuous soon after that. Since we couldn't easily make 100,000 yen just by selling rice, we were lucky that the manager of the farm cooperative happened to be a friend of Sensei's, so we were able to get a small loan.

The group from Kagawa included one man who said he had had some experience in making tatami. But he wasn't much help, so the young people took their lunch boxes and went out to observe the tatami shops here and there. At the ones nearby, the people were afraid we had become a competitor. They panicked, and did not like the idea of teaching us; so we practically had to steal looks at the process. Even so, by imitating what we had seen, we got the straw through the innards of the machine somehow or other, and a mat actually began to take shape. Once twenty or thirty mats had accumulated, we piled them on the cart that went for the morning garbage in Haibara, took them to the station and stacked them in a baggage car. The baggage agent let us ride along free. Of course as we took the mats, we did not forget to conceal on ourselves an inconspicuous amount of rice. The mats weren't likely to be exchanged for cash right away, and there were deadlines for the interest on the loan. So we had to black-market to get cash for paying the interest too.

When we arrived at Ueroku station in Osaka, Yamanaka borrowed a cart from the express agency. We went along the hilly street between Ueroku and Tanimachi, Yamanaka pulling on the handle and Sensei pushing from the rear. I followed after at a half-trot. We went around that way hunting for a tatami dealer who might buy from us. We did not have any special place in mind; whenever we saw a tatami shop we would rush in and try to deal with them. But a man who is a professional dealer doesn't have any reason to buy goods that suddenly turn up and that he knows at a glance are the work of amateurs. "We can't just dump these and go home," grumbled Yamanaka. We must have gone a long way by then. Our bodies were tired, and worse than that our spirits were crushed. But we didn't give up; we kept looking for a place, trying to encourage each other, walking on pulling and pushing the cart.

In this way we eventually came to a dealer's where— although we felt miserable about leaning on the sympathy of one of the workmen—the price we got for our mats was just a little better than if we had sold the straw without processing it. In any case, we had sold the goods. We came back to Shinkyō cheering each other with the thought that we could put up with the poorest prices for a while in order to practice the trade, and that one day we would show them that we had become regular professionals.

A number of times after that too, we had poorly made tatami taken off our hands thanks to the workman's good will. Then one day he suddenly came out to Shinkyō and said he had quit that shop; couldn't we use him at our place? We had to tell him our standard of living did not leave us any margin for hiring others. Then, I don't know how it happened, but a number of mats that had been propped up where he was standing fell over on top of him. He was unable to get up, and there was great commotion over calling a doctor. The doctor ordered a three-month rest. So in that way the man came to live at Shinkyō after all. Everybody did their best to nurse him. The doctor said, "You ought to be glad; you had a lucky accident, and your limp is cured." He meant that the crippled leg had gone back to where it originally had been, thanks to having been pinned under the mats. When his injuries had healed, he brought in a girlfriend from somewhere and said he wanted to live at Shinkyō for the rest of his life. But the second day she was there she said, "Communal life is awful," and persuaded him to go away.

Gradually this straw-weaving and mat-making, which we had begun part-time along with our farming, became more productive, and our technique improved; soon the straw from our own fields was far from being enough and we had to lay in a supply from other farms. In 1949, after looking the situation over carefully, the co-op advanced us 100,000 yen to buy raw materials on credit.

It probably was because the co-op president had faith in his friend Ozaki rather than because he had faith in Shinkyō. But since he continued to accommodate us with capital for raw materials—300,000 yen the second time, 500,000 yen the third time—our financial situation was greatly eased, and we had even more encouragement to work. We always repaid it at the end of each year. That was why Shinkyō's credit rating went way up.

In the fall of 1950 typhoon Jane caused a good deal of damage in the Osaka region. The tatami dealers who were our regular customers found their stocks completely water-logged. When he saw it, Sensei said, "The trouble is mutual. Unless we can get you back on your feet, Shinkyō won't get back on its feet. In this case we don't think we should take any money from you for these damaged mats." He refused payment, and that seems to have won him a reputation for being unusually considerate for this day and age.

"Three years after the foundation," the saying goes. By about then Shinkyō's tatami had four or five regular dealers and had managed to become regular commercial goods. At Shinkyō we put the maker's name into every mat; that way we got our dealers to make complaints by name if by any chance the goods were poorly constructed.

It not only helps us improve our technique, it seems to have improved our dealers' confidence. Perhaps our business methods were not very up-to-date, but it was because we wanted to do everything in simple good faith.

Many houses were blown down or washed away by wind and water from the typhoon, and because of it there was a rush on building materials. Since that includes tatami, if we had wanted to we probably could have ridden the waves of price increases and gotten ourselves a good profit. Our dealers urged us to raise our prices a little each time, but Sensei and all of us insisted, "You want to raise prices at a time when people have been struck by natural disaster, but we just can't do it. We are basically farmers, and we can always manage to get something to eat, even if it is at the lowest standard of living. We won't raise prices just because of the situation now." We figured it did not matter to us if they thought we were stubborn. In fact maybe that was better: so many orders came from this or that dealer who had heard about what we said that we could not possibly fill them at our previous rate of production.

At that point the co-op again came to our aid. They said they would loan us one million yen to buy more machinery. We borrowed it at once. Of course, as usual it was all paid back at the end of the year. The following year the co-op loaned us two million yen. The number of machines increased from two to three to four. And by this time Shinkyō itself had become one of the co-op's best customers.

CHAPTER ELEVEN
Trial after trial

I had suffered deep but invisible wounds because of my stay in jail. I was thirty-eight, and had reached full maturity as a woman; but I felt that through this experience I had discovered how little I knew of the world and how much I still was like an infant.

Even after the affair was over and done with, my sense of gloom didn't clear up. When I asked Sensei, "Don't you have any feelings about what the evacuees did to you?" and he answered, "I don't think anything of it," I couldn't help being irked. And even if I forgot about the evacuees, what Yamanaka had said always would echo in my heart. It was when the police had arrested us that last time for selling black-market rice, and later threatened us with a fine of 100,000 yen. Yamanaka was saying we couldn't possibly pay a hundred thousand in cash, so why didn't we work it off at hard labor instead? "It isn't as though we are out to make money," he said to us, "so how about getting Sensei to take a labor sentence?"

From Yamanaka's point of view there was no ill will in this. Besides, he was desperate to save Shinkyō. But from my point of view his words sounded utterly cruel, and I really hated him. Sensei, however, seemed amazingly calm.

"Yamanaka is the one who worries most about Shinkyō's finances, so what he said is no surprise. Anyway, he is right. The way our finances are now we haven't got that kind of money; and since the rest of you all are better at the farm work than I am, I'm the most appropriate one to go work off the fine."

He was so casual about it he seemed to be saying he didn't even mind going to prison. In the end the issue dissolved, as I've already told you. But as far as I was concerned that did not mean a period had been put on the episode at all.

I was in indescribable pain. I was suffering from disillusion. No, worse than that: I no longer was able to grasp Sensei's feelings. No matter how hard I tried, I wasn't able to take a far-sighted view like his of not distrusting people. Had my heart and his actually gone off in separate ways? Are the travels of the heart nothing but lonely ones after all?

While I was carrying on this way great changes surged in upon our communal life. Our membership grew steadily. New people joined via one contact or another and for all sorts of reasons—spiritual training, family situation, disaster, repatriation. We took them in without setting any restrictions or particularly keeping an eye on them. It wasn't that I could not understand why Sensei felt that way. But no matter how generous and lenient Sensei and the rest of us meant to be, you just couldn't expect all the people who joined us to be decent.

We can forget about those who came because of spiritual longings. But the repatriates, the sufferers, and those who came because of other material motives—in short those who came only because they hungered for bread and just planned to use Shinkyō for a while—such people didn't stay long, and once their bellies were full they would go away without even a thank-you. Some of them tipped us by stealing our money and goods, or by using the Shinkyō name to work frauds outside. The cleverest case of all was that of a man who went away, and after a few days came back with partners to rob us; they stole a lot of the rationed cloth everybody had carefully been saving.

As events like that began to pile up, I lost all my innocence. It got to where I just could not trust people any more. Not only strangers; I didn't even trust Sensei. I began to feel that maybe it was not such a good idea to leave this precious communal way of life in the hands of such an easygoing Sensei. I particularly couldn't help getting angry when Sensei and Yamanaka never once took precautions, even after they had been tricked many times by smooth-tongued sharpies. This happened, for instance:

In 1950 we needed to move the Storehouse and wanted to build new foundations with concrete, which still was not easy to get. One day a man came to inspect us, saying he was from the Ministry of Agriculture and Forestry, "Do you want me to get you a supply of concrete?" he asked. Greed breeds eagerness. We slid into it carelessly and nobody was a bit suspicious, so we handed him thirty-some thousand yen as earnest money. Afterward when we realized we had been taken, Sensei simply tossed it off by saying, "That man pulled a good one on us, didn't he?" But my heart was pounding with anger. Yes, too bad we were cheated; but Sensei's attitude, pitiable or enviable as it might be, was no laughing matter. That was not all. The swindler was caught, but he made more trouble for us by making wild statements about how we had entertained and bribed him— all said to make himself look better. Even then Sensei said only, "I'm not going to make any excuses to the police. He is a human being; if he hears that we were put in jail because of his lies, he'll be sure to have second thoughts." I begged Sensei to please go to the police and explain it properly; no, not explain, just tell the truth. I argued with him that after all he had to establish our own innocence, for one thing. And furthermore that while he was talking about saving a man who had gone wrong, it was senseless to try to do so without using judgment—doesn't love for people force us to use a whip sometimes? Not that I didn't understand his feelings; no, I understood them so well that more and more I was ceasing to understand them.

Another time had been in August, 1948. It was when our tatami work had finally gotten onto the tracks. Yamanaka was delivering mats, and on the way back, as the truck was running down a street in Yao, it hit a bus and crushed the arm of a middle-aged passenger who had stuck it out a window. The passenger filed a claim against both Shinkyō and the bus company for well over two million yen. The company's accident specialist came and got them off the hook with glib talk, so Shinkyō had to take all the blame. It was utterly idiotic.

If things like this went on, we would be done for. I picked quarrels with Sensei and tried on purpose to annoy him. "Sensei, what do you suppose I should do about the way I feel? You used to be a missionary, so why don't you save me from this feeling that I cannot trust people anymore? What do I have to do to reach that state where I will be at peace with the world?"

"There isn't anything I can teach you. There are things I want to learn from you."

"Are you making fun of me?" There wasn't a bit of ridicule in what he said, of course. That I knew. I knew it, but somehow I was unbearably annoyed.

"I envy you your attitude. Don't you ever give any thought to what will happen to Shinkyō in the future?"

"The future?" he replied. "You can think about it but there's nothing you can do about it, is there?"

"But aren't you concerned about what will happen to the members after you are dead? When I think about it, I cannot settle down," I said.

"After I am dead? After you die, you can't see anything. Who knows?"

"Aren't you being too irresponsible?"

"Oh, enough of that," he said. "Think about Shinkyō's affairs after I'm dead? I'm not smart enough to do that, knowing I have to die some day anyway."

We went over the same topics day after day.

By the time the doctor diagnosed it as nervous prostration, my symptoms were pretty well advanced. Physical weakling that I am, my mind and nerves don't seem to be very strong. There is no illness as painful to a person as this one is—although nobody else can see exactly what is wrong. In the beginning, while I was thinking my stomach must be bad or maybe my heart had gotten weak, I got so I could hardly walk, and my head felt as heavy as if I had three steel helmets on it. Being left alone threw me into such anxiety I could not bear it. Breathing was difficult.

I clung to Sensei and would not part from him for even a moment. When he asked me what I was afraid of, I couldn't answer. People's faces would appear around me at random, and I had a feeling that little sounds were echoing inside me. I struggled to save the precious bit of self-control still left in me. If I lost it, I would certainly go mad.

Everybody was good about bringing me my three meals; but when I put anything into my mouth, I couldn't breathe, and then when I tried to breathe I couldn't eat—so it took real effort just to get through a meal.

Half a month passed this way, then twenty days. All that time I hardly ever slept a wink. It was during the hottest part of the summer of 1951. On the twentieth night, as usual I wasn't actually thinking but just sitting in a fog, when all of a sudden something flashed. I jumped, and my body went cold. What an idiot to have been so self-centered! For twenty days I had not done a thing, I had just been wrapped up in my own illness and had thoughtlessly given the others a hard time. And yet daily life at Shinkyō was going on steadily and continuously, wasn't it? Why was I so fond of agonizing about the future? Wasn't it conceited, malicious, a delusion, a heart going contrary to nature? Not being able to trust people must mean your sense of gratitude to them is inadequate. Everybody, no matter who he is, has points of strength and beauty. If you do not have a sense of gratitude, you obviously do not think well enough of others. So worrying about what would happen after Sensei and I died was nothing but a form of self-conceit. It was a sign of an eagerness to impose my will on others, wasn't it? And that surely was unreasonable and unnatural. At the time we were ostracized, did anybody foresee our present way of life? If that's the case, then in the same way nobody can know what might happen in the future. Finally even I understood the state of mind I had fallen into. And at the same time I began to understand Sensei's feelings again.

I no longer needed medicines or shots. Whenever I got afraid of dying, I would remind myself that there was nothing I could do about it anyway, that our human powers are not enough to let us fathom whether we are going to live or die. When I staggered up out of bed, everybody was so surprised they tried to hold me down. But I stubbornly threw them off. Not having slept much for twenty days, I ached when I went to work cleaning and laundering; my body seemed about to collapse, but I gritted my teeth and forced it on.

I revealed to no one, not even Sensei, that my mind's eye had been opened. But from that day on I began a new kind of fight against disease. My illness grew a little better each day. The truth is that it was a long time before I recovered completely. But for me it was a second rebirth.

In 1948 we built a tatami plant of 370 *tsubo* [one tsubo is 3.95 square yards]; in 1949 a bathhouse and dressing room with six bedrooms on the second floor; and in 1953 we moved the Storehouse and built a second tatami shop of 160 tsubo. At the time we had three trucks. Unexpectedly, however, the Storehouse and the 370-tsubo shop were blown down by typhoon #13 on September 25, 1953, with massive damage to goods and machinery. The loss totalled seven million yen.

Although we had made relatively regular progress, when this disaster came, we were told that outsiders thought we couldn't recover in less than three years. However, we were not badly demoralized; in fact, we didn't have time to be demoralized. If we did not hurry and rebuild, we would starve to death because we had nothing to fall back on. In short, we were fighting with our backs to the water.

The very next morning we began to struggle with the task of reconstruction. We regretted even having to take time to receive people who came to offer condolences. We collected usable-looking parts, and by putting them together we managed to build two good tatami machines. The following day we began production day and night, in shifts, working out-of-doors. Until the typhoon hit us we had had five machines and a daily output of two hundred mats, and we regained the same rate once we got back into action with only two machines but working two shifts. So we did not inconvenience our dealers in the slightest. I don't know the exact figure, but at that time our yearly income from tatami was about three million yen. Besides operating the machines, we plugged right along at rebuilding the shop. The village people seemed dazzled by the power of our collective effort. Anyway, we were back on our feet in just a few months' time.

Everything would be great if life went along without upset, but you cannot expect that. From the beginning of 1954 Shinkyō was caught in the whirlpool of the consolidation of town and village administrations, and it turned out to be a real mess.

Kasama originally had been in Kijō county, so the village mayors from Kijō came over and urged us to join them in consolidating with the town of Sakurai, while people came out from Haibara town hall and urged us to join with *them*. Of course the Kasama villagers were of several minds. Ever since the ostracizing in 1937, none of us had been allowed in a village meeting, and we were placed outside the regular village administrative channels just as though we were a separate hamlet. But when it came to a major issue

like this consolidation even Shinkyō could not remain indifferent, and Sensei went to a village meeting for the first
time.

Most of the people tended to favor consolidating with
Haibara, but they were unwilling to say so openly because
they had not been able to gauge the bosses' opinion. Sensei's
stand was a blank to them, so both sides tried to win him
over. First, five or six of the Seki gang came to Shinkyō and
lured him by saying, "We're undecided about it, and whatever you think is all right with us; all we want you to do is
serve as midwife for the operation." Then they secretly
sent some ordinary villagers to ask Sensei to agree to consolidating with Haibara. When he got to the meeting, he
realized that the Seki gang, though they said they were undecided, really meant to use his stand to coax the villagers

over to the Sakurai side. Once he had caught on to their scheming and double-dealing, he said that since this wasn't an issue that could be settled by majority vote and that every man's views should be heard, he turned to the people and began to ask them one by one, "Sakurai or Haibara—which do you choose, and what is your reason?"

The advantages of Haibara were that the town hall would be closer, the middle school would be closer, customs and attitudes matched ours well, the village was adjacent to Uda county (which included Haibara), and the shopping district would be more convenient. The Sakurai side argued that taxes would be lower there, and that although the middle school was a long way it would actually be closer if we organized a school bus. The people who supported Haibara were hesitant in front of bosses who favored Sakurai, so they did not state any very concrete reasons for their choice. They were caught between public and private pressures.

At first the count stood six to four in favor of Haibara, then seven to three. And as Sensei went on questioning them one by one, the Sakurai side gradually decreased until at last it was reduced to one man. That took three months, from January into March. Sensei held a general village meeting almost every night. Quite a few on the Haibara side urged him, "Why not forget about the one man left and declare a consolidation with Haibara? It is all right to be considerate, but is this going to go on forever?" But Sensei was being extra careful and did not want to end by treating the holdout unfairly. Actually, the fact was that the man did not have any real reason for holding out; he did it only because the bosses had told him to, and now he had gone so far he was afraid to back down. When Sensei then asked the villagers what they thought should be done about the man, they all said he should be left in the cold. When he heard that, he looked up in surprise and at once reversed his decision. And so in the end, thanks to Sensei's midwifery, the decision was reached with literally unanimous agreement.

The consolidation ceremony was held in August of 1954 in Haibara. The mayor turned to Sensei as the man who had worked hardest for it, and said, "Please state your conditions for consolidating." The village had left this to Sensei's discretion, and he answered, "Unconditional." The mayor said, "I can't accept that. 'Having no policy is the strongest policy,' and even though you say 'unconditional,' we all know that a matter such as this cannot be settled without conditions. Your tactics frighten me." And so it came about that in response to our "unconditional" conditions the mayor agreed to rebuild Kasama's dilapidated primary school and repair the eroded riverbanks in the village.

Not long after the consolidation, Seki Iwazō entered the town hospital because of a stomach ulcer, and Sensei and I helped take him there. By this time he had had one misfortune after another; his monopoly on village power had crumbled, and he was only a shadow of his former self. We had come to feel sorry for him.

For some months Sensei was involved in arrangements for the new school building. The work went along surprisingly smoothly, and the dedication ceremony was held on April 17, 1956. Shinkyō provided meals for the carpenters, painters, plasterers and laborers; and we advanced money for construction costs and other expenses.

On the matter of riverbank repairs, though, there was opposition. The reason, of course, was that "If the river is widened, I will be in trouble because I will lose some paddy." Since there *was* some material basis for the argument, it could not be rejected bluntly. But we soon realized that behind it there were strings being pulled by the Seki faction, who were playing tricks out of spite because Haibara had won. So in order to forestall opposition, Shinkyō borrowed some thirty thousand yen from the co-op and compensated the owners of the paddies that would be damaged. With that their reason for opposition vanished, and with the consent of all parties the decision was made to begin the first phase of the work in 1956.

On March 3rd the work was begun, and the following year the second phase was undertaken. During the interim we had news that really warmed our hearts. It was that those who have paddies along the river found they now could go through a rainstorm without worrying about sand damage. It meant that the loss of a little paddy had brought them such a boon that there was nothing to complain about; and those who had gotten compensation from Shinkyō the previous year now sent it back via the District Chief.

[The village had become a district of the town of Haibara, and so now had a "district chief" rather than a "headman" as its highest administrative officer and representative on the town council.]

When the second phase was finished, Sensei donated some of Shinkyō's paddy and had the main village road widened as far as the river. Until then, people who wanted to go to fields across the river had to carry everything on their shoulders, but with the dikes and the road widened they could use rubber-tired carts.

Sensei questioned one of the men who had opposed the repairs. "You knew how good this would be, so why did you work against it?" The man shook his head, "I didn't have any reason for it."

"With the nation and the prefecture ready to give ten million and more yen to a little village like this, how could you *not* think about it carefully? You had no business opposing it without any reason."

We just had time for a breather, when problems of village administration came up again. It involved the contest for District Chief.

Up to now, the power-holders had been concentrated in the central section, partly because it had the largest population. But the consolidation made people realize how inconvenient it would be if certain village practices continued as before. And so the issue of the Chief's job grew complicated. No matter who took it on, an opposition group would campaign secretly and drag him down, so that finally nobody wanted the post any more. The town mayor was annoyed because he had no one to contact in the village. The result was that he came to talk "non-partisan" Ozaki Sensei into taking on the responsibility. Sensei reflected on it indecisively for some days, then eventually resolved to do it. At a village meeting he declared:

"I did not become Chief because anybody nominated me. I have taken the job on my own. I am not going to give three bows and nine bows and say, 'Please, I beg to have your consideration and your freely given vote.' If a man truly is concerned for his country and his village, then the right thing for him to do is willingly to come out and take responsibility for them. I don't have any special ambitions. Those of you who have been serving as neighborhood group leaders up to now, if you are willing to cooperate with me as Chief I would like to have you. And if you dislike the idea, it is all right with me if all of you refuse. I can do it by myself if I have to."

All of them said, almost in unison, that they would work with him, and they bowed their heads. And so Sensei became District Chief in September, 1957.

On October 9th of the following year, when we were just about to leave for a general meeting, the leaders of neighborhood groups #1 and #2 in the central section came over. "The central section wants to be absent from tonight's meeting," they said. So the Seki faction was challenging Sensei again. But he didn't move or color at all. "So you're leaving the village? All right, it is settled." The two messengers looked sort of surprised. But Sensei left it at that and went off to the meeting as though nothing had happened.

At the start of the meeting Sensei made this casual statement: "The central section seems to be leaving the village for the night. I don't know where they are going to stay, but if all of them go sleep someplace else, that will be amusing. I told them if they could not stand their Chief or if something was going wrong, I would talk it over all they wanted. However, if they want to get out of the village, I will not try to stop them just because it is inconvenient for me; I let them go. Now if there is anybody else who wants out, you needn't be bashful, you can speak up." Naturally with everybody from central absent the meeting blossomed into a discussion of them instead of the main order of business.

Some days later came the festival of the village guardian gods. As one of the regular events, everybody scatters ricecakes around the shrine grounds on the eve of the main celebration. However, this time some of the villagers said we shouldn't pick up any ricecakes thrown by the central people. When they heard about it, the central people sneaked to the shrine and back again before the general procession began. Then, in order to get even, the western people raised their paper lanterns high on their poles, formed a line, and instead of joining with central they marched right on through, shouting all the way to the shrine grounds. East formed up behind Sensei and marched in next.

The central people felt a sense of desertion that they had never known before. They came to Sensei to offer apologies. He said, "It is not my nature to accept apologies. When you said you all were leaving the village, I could only say okay. And now when you say you are coming back into the village, I can only say okay." That was the case; the central group, as you might expect, did not even try to respond beyond just lowering their heads in shame. Sensei went on with a laugh, "In the old days at the beginning of the ostracism the central people treated us badly. But twenty years have passed, and now you have been ostracized by your own choice. I guess you know just a little of how it feels, right?"

What a victory it was! This happened in October, 1958.

Sensei sat in the Chief's seat in 1958, 1959 and 1960; and he not only put his energy into serving as family counsellor and go-between, he also worked hard to have the main village road widened. Because of him, gradually the map of the village began to change.

But bad news follows good, they say, and calamity struck us. It was the Shinkyō fire of February 25, 1960.

Sensei and five or six of us were at the Osaka office. It is at 1-chōme, Nishi-ku; we set it up in 1957 and since then have taken turns manning it. It serves as a contact point for our dealers; and our delivery truck drivers stop there to take meals and to run errands. For the rest of us the office is a window where from time to time we can come into contact with the urban atmosphere of Osaka. On the 25th everybody had taken the day off and gone to Osaka for movies and sightseeing, had had lunch and gone home. Only Sensei and a few others still were there.

Then a phone call came. Kimiyo, the duty cook, said tearfully, "Shinkyō's on fire! The Workshop and Food Storehouse are blazing away! Hurry and come back!"

We dropped everything and flew out to the truck. We drove as fast as was legal, and by the time we came over Onnayori Pass, we could see that the Workshop roof already had completely caved in. Sensei was saying it was bad enough that Shinkyō was burning but what he was really afraid of was that the fire had spread to the neighbor's; however, it looked as though Otani's place was safe, so he felt a little better.

From time to time straw processors had told us that when straw catches fire it goes off like gunpowder, but we still hadn't thought a building could burn down so fast. The sight of a 370-tsubo building completely ablaze is a real spectacle. I didn't seem to have any feelings about how weird and sad it was. Those who were working as hard as they could to put out the fire may take me wrong, but that was honestly how I felt. As our truck stopped, women of the village women's league came up around us and said, "It's really something, isn't it?" With the roof fallen down on top of it, the mound of straw piled inside was fiercely shooting sparks in all directions.

The entire town fire brigade was there, about five hundred of them crowding around the scene. All eight pumpers from Haibara were there too.

I threaded my way through the wall of people and raced up to the kitchen. There I found members of the Haibara women's league, the Tokiwa league, and others who had hurried over to offer condolences, and who had brought a mound of canned goods and riceballs. Kimiyo's eyes were red from crying, and Shigeno was pallid and stood there stiffly erect. They said the Kasama women's league had divided up the work and was making emergency rations— lunches for us and riceballs for five hundred firemen.

The sun sets early in winter, and some time or other everything around us had gotten dark, but at the scene of the fire it was like midday, the blaze burned on so brightly. I heard that somebody from the village was in the garage up above the road serving as receptionist for condolence callers; and when I went to see, uniformed police were keeping people in line, the reception room was lined with condolence bottles of sake, and Kosaka (leader of neighborhood group #1 in the eastern section) was in charge.

Even around there a lot of village men were standing fire watch. After all, since they could not do anything with the blaze itself, they might at least keep it from spreading. I greeted the receptionists and the villagers and went back to the kitchen again.

The police said they wanted to borrow a place where

they could begin questioning people about the situation when the fire was discovered, so I opened several rooms and brought braziers and tea. They divided up and questioned people, but some said it spread from the west, some from the east, and some said the whole thing went up in flames at once; so it wasn't easy to get at the cause.

Nobody slept a wink that night, and a hundred firemen stayed and kept guard. Next morning the neighborhood group leaders divided up the territory and went off to make rounds of all the houses, thanking people for bringing condolences the day before. That day we moved the reception desk to the kitchen entrance. Kosaka again served as receptionist, and the callers kept coming from morning to night without a break. People we knew well would come up into the tatami-floor lounge and sit around talking with Sensei. Apparently the fire had been reported by the radio and the press, and callers came day and night so constantly that we hardly had time enough to think.

The night of the fire I remembered that I would have to order new machinery, so I called manufacturers in Nagoya and Hyōgo.

We were so incredibly busy we would get dizzy, but as the worst of the shock began to fade, whenever Shinkyō people came together they agreed, "It is really a good thing Sensei wasn't here when the fire broke out. With his temperament he might have jumped right in and been burned to death." So it was lucky he was in the Osaka office. What worried him so much, more than anything else, was that the fire might spread next door; and apparently he was determined that if it happened, he could not bear to live. That's why when we looked ahead from Onnayori Pass and realized it hadn't spread, he automatically said "Ah, good." And after we got to the scene, all he kept saying was, "I'm really glad Kosaka was saved." In fact, these words brought on doubts about us when the cause of the fire was investigated.

As the fruits of our labor burned away until none were

left, even Sensei seemed ready to accept the idea that it was the end of Shinkyō. However, among the condolence callers there was a tatami wholesaler from Nagoya, and he said that on the way over he had met another man in the trade who told him, "Shinkyō burned down—hooray for us!" and gloated over a rival's misfortune. When he heard that, Sensei jumped straight up. "Oh, yes? If that's what they're saying, we will definitely reopen our business and show them what we can do!" It had been quite a while since we had seen that expression on his face—bursting with energy and ready to fight. The old Ozaki spirit had come back. When the members heard what he had said, the words really braced them up. Shinkyō wasn't going to be badly beaten on account of a fire. So we went right out to where a lot of villagers were helping clean up the debris, and asked them to excuse us from helping them but we wanted to get at the work of rebuilding right away. The villagers and condolence callers seemed caught off guard a little by our eagerness.

The day after the fire, while it still was smouldering, we stopped cleaning up and had six carpenters come out and get to work. They were to build us a temporary shop. They were so full of enthusiasm they said they would have the ridgepole up by March 5th. The third day after the fire, the machines arrived. They had been meant for other places but were quickly switched and sent to us. We began to operate them day and night in three-man shifts.

Even a week later the flames burned on. For three days in a row Kosaka wrote seven hundred cards of thanks to the firemen and others, all the while serving as receptionist. On March 7th and 8th teams of about thirty people each came by turns from the three sections of the village and finished cleaning up. In the end, the strawpile smouldered on for nearly a month. On the blistered and still hot ground the six carpenters went steadily ahead with the new Workshop and Storehouse.

We were really grateful that money would be coming

in from our fire insurance, even though it wouldn't be much because unluckily we had just reduced the premium that year. Happily, by April 10th we had worked our way to a point where we were able to announce our revival and at the same time offer a round of thanks. We sent invitations to more than five hundred people who had brought condolence gifts, and the day before the celebration, members of the village women's league helped us make box lunches enough for four hundred guests.

The first Sunday after the fire Sensei said, "We can't have people thinking 'Shinkyō's lost its nerve' just because of a fire, so why don't we take the day off like we always have on Sunday?" But one of the young men objected: "Uncle, what are you saying? With the carpenters and village people here working, what will they think if we do that? Can't we do without Sundays until after the revival celebration?" The way the young people worked was astounding. Running the machines, cleaning up debris, helping the carpenters, they kept at it without a break. And we were touched when the primary-school children said, "You talked about buying us canvas shoes, but because of the fire we don't have to have them."

The day before the celebration the six carpenters put together an outdoor stage and set up tents to use for a raffle-stand and for handing out lunches. Unfortunately the weather that day was bad, and the red and white ceremonial arch was wet with rain as it greeted the guests. Receiving lines were set up alphabetically, and fourteen people shared reception duty. People divided up the tasks—taking charge of the stage show, the rest area, the raffle—and that meant using not only Shinkyō members of course but also the neighborhood group leaders and the officers of the women's league.

The Cadillac of the president of Yanmar Diesel Corporation bored through the arch and came up the hill. Seven or eight private cars were lined up by the arch, and taxis came and went endlessly. There also was a special bus making many round trips from Haibara. The guests looked at the new plant and storehouse and were astonished by the speed of our recovery.

The investigation into the cause of the fire took a surprisingly long time. As I mentioned, they thought it funny that Sensei was so concerned about the neighbors' places, and I think they secretly suspected us of arson in order to get the insurance money. And when the eyewitnesses all gave different testimony, the inspectors' suspicions grew deeper. Of course they also checked out other possibilities. However Sensei took the lead, and while we were searching the ruins where we thought the fire had started, we made a great discovery. In one part of the area where straw and supplies had been piled, a hole had been gouged out fairly deeply and about fifty centimeters in diameter. The ashes right above it were white and almost completely burnt; the next ones above them were burnt black; and above those, half-black, in layers. It meant that the lowest layer had ignited by spontaneous combustion and had burned for quite a while; then as the fire gradually rose it finally flamed up, and sparks were spewed almost explosively as though from a fifty centimeter pipe. By the time the flames were spotted, fire had completely spread through the bottom layer. Apparently spontaneous combustion cases like this are unusual. Discovering the cause did not bring back what we had lost, but we were relieved that at least that queer and foggy suspicion had fully been swept away.

CHAPTER TWELVE

A new Eve

Twenty years after we were ostracized the positions were reversed. The faction that drove us out had gradually lost its power; Sensei had become District Chief; and Shinkyō's existence was recognized, which means we had established a base from which we neither would move nor be moved. Because Sensei now was Chief, many evil customs and senseless conventions in the village were corrected. And one of the most significant of these had to do with the Eve.

Because Sensei and the four families were excluded from participating in activities at the guardian shrine even though they too were children of the gods, they had no way of knowing the details of how the celebrations were done. This was especially true for the Eve. We learned that at some time or other the evacuees and the so-called poor people of the village had been held unqualified to participate. That is, during the Eve they did not have equal standing with the rest of the village. Sensei was furious about the injustice of it. Things like this would not make the guardian gods happy, he said; and he wanted to arrange it so that everybody in the village, rich or poor, could wholeheartedly join in the celebration. So he revised the entire procedure.

The custom had been that in each section a family that had been chosen by lot for that year would invite everybody from the section, make more ricecakes than could be eaten, and prepare a feast. To welcome their guests properly, they would put down new tatami, buy new utensils, and repair the house. The money spent for this purpose could run to forty or fifty thousand yen per family, so that the village as a whole lost 200,000 yen every year just because of the Eve. That is why it wasn't quite so unreasonable for evacuees and poor people not to take part.

The lots were drawn in the shrine grounds on the day of the Eve. Everybody was timid while drawing them. They all would be thinking "It would be better if I could win some other year." If they did happen to win, they would say, "Ah, what luck; I'm so thankful." But as they regretfully accepted the lots their faces carried tearful smiles. Nevertheless, it still was better than being an "unincluded" person: one not allowed to take part.

I planned a meal for that day that would cost eighty yen per person. For sixty people [one from each household] that came to 4800 yen. This was the total cost of the village-wide Eve this time. We prepared the food in Shinkyō's kitchen, with eager help from the seven neighborhood group leaders. When the food was ready, it was carried to the shrine in a Shinkyō truck. One after another the village people carried it up the sixty-six steps of the stone stairway. And when they were done the ceremony began.

The shrine committee urged Sensei to take the seat of honor. But he said, "It is stupid the way things have been done. We cannot have the Chief in the top seat on each and every occasion. Since this affair is for the guardians, the right thing is to have the shrine committee sit there." Even in trivial matters like this Sensei's senses were operating.

The ceremony was simple. When it was done the sixty of them went up to the worship hall and sat down with their eighty-yen feast in front of them. They sat in rows facing each other, not separated into rich and poor, and including all those who had been left out until then. A young couple who had been married just a few days earlier were made to sit in the Chief's seat and had their marriage officially announced by Sensei. The couple, their parents, and

the village people all seemed to appreciate his considerate-
ness. The ruddy-cheeked young bridegroom was the
adopted heir of a Kasama house. Village practice had been
to slight an adopted heir. The saying was, "If it is a face
you don't recognize, it must be somebody's adopted heir";
and he was looked down upon as being a grade lower than
other men. Sensei had taken a cut at this crude old custom.

He explained tactfully, "The family arranged a simpli-
fied wedding, as I asked them to, and will not give return
presents to everybody in the village, but instead offers these
five bottles of sake and would like everybody to drink them
together this Eve. Along with introducing the principals,
I am introducing the sake. That is why there won't be any
furoshiki and *manjū* [bean-jam buns] delivered to your
houses." And with that the adopted heir had officially been
welcomed into village membership.

With the banquet over, the main event of the Eve, the
otowatashi, ["passing the duty"] began. When Sensei
directed, the shrine committee went up to the altar, and
standing outside in a drizzle everybody bowed for the worship ceremony. By custom the three men chosen by lot for
the year would carry part of the sacred objects home; it
meant that in addition to worshipping them at home, the
three also were responsible for keeping the shrine grounds
clean that year. When the next Eve came they would turn
over these duties and objects to the new team, i.e., to the
ones newly chosen in the lottery drawn before the gods. The
shrine committee faced the old team, bowed their heads, and
said, "You have served the gods well this year." The old
team sat by the west side of the altar, and the new team
opposite them on the east. Next the committee faced the
new team and greeted them, "We ask you to serve the gods
for the coming year."

Oddly enough, the three who had drawn lots for the
coming year all were men who had just been allowed to

take part in the Eve for the first time. It was a happy chance because all three might otherwise have gone through life and never once been up by the altar.

There is no doubt that the new-style Eve celebration made a deep impression on the village people. One of the three on the new team said, "Nothing could be as welcome as this. Gentlemen of the committee, I thank you. I will guard the gods as though my life depended on it." And he went away light-hearted. Sensei said to the people, "The gods are impartial. Mysterious, isn't it, that all three of these men, each from a different section, each a man who had been 'unincluded' until now, were chosen this time?"

This way, no matter who was chosen, it would not cost them a cent for expenses. Furthermore the whole village would celebrate as equals, and nobody would be offended. The Eve of 1959 had ended dramatically. And a long-traditional custom had been revolutionized in one swoop.

The unintentional utopia

The years since the new Eve have been good ones for Ozaki Sensei and the people of Shinkyō. Their factory is now the largest tatami-making establishment in the nation, and their daily life is, by rural Japanese standards, affluent. Many of their countrymen admire them as a success, and quite a few regard them as a model for collectivization and rural regeneration.

The building of Shinkyō offers many lessons for those concerned with community development and cultural activism, but like any good case history it can be studied from various points of view. My own craft is ethnography, a special branch of reporting; and an ethnographer's first duty is to provide cultural translation. Verbal translation is a part of it, as in the preceding chapters; whole domains of life in other cultures remain unknown and undocumented despite the abundance of some kinds of information that we have about a people such as the Japanese. But the greater duty is—to use the slang phrase—to bring 'em back alive. This does not mean to cage them as specimens in an ethnic zoo; it means to show them as men and women who happen to be in a unique and (to us) exotic environment and who are struggling for a better life in ways that are utterly human.

As humans we strive to re-shape our parochial traditions at the same time that we are being shaped by them. Ozaki and the building of his commune exemplify both aspects of the process. The values, themes and behavior patterns we see in Shinkyō are, each taken by itself, within the range of options that a rural Japanese would find acceptable, even desirable; part of a good way of life. In this sense Shinkyō can serve as a sample of Japanese popular tradition, although obviously it is not a statistician's random or averaged sample. But Ozaki and his group also have taken parts from the common cultural repertoire and have replayed them in ways that both they and their countrymen recognize to be new and different. And in this sense the Shinkyō case can also serve as a useful measure (though an incomplete one) of what the rural Japanese recognize as ideal, as not just a good way of life but potentially a better one.

The ethnologist's occupational disease is to become addicted to showing how traditions—cultural grammars of behavior, thought, and feeling—condition people in any setting. To be sure, this is a fact of the human condition: we are born speechless and survive only by learning the local idiom. It is also a fact that we are in some degree, depending on our talents, word-makers as well as word-mongers. And I believe that ethnology must also begin to account as well for these creative rhetorics of behavior that, like wit, overcome the limits of grammar in the very act of using it. One little ethnographic case will not do it; we will need many. We will also need new concepts and theories of kinds that I, at least, can scarcely forecast. What I can do is examine the Shinkyō experience in terms of its inventiveness as well as its typical-ness, and try to show some of the ways in which it is simultaneously a manifestation of and a reaction against Japanese rural tradition.

I am not a native of rural Japan, much less of Shinkyō, although I have devoted much of the past decade to studying and investigating various domains of Japanese life. My experiences, purposes, and perspectives all differ from those of Mrs. Sugihara; as a by-product you may find it amusing to contrast my outsider's views with hers as a "true believer." My own examination of Shinkyō rests partly on her narrative but also on several visits I made to Shinkyō in the spring and summer of 1965 and again in the summer of 1966. This was far too little time for me to become an insider in any real sense. It was enough time, though, for me to be able to see Ozaki and the group in action in an array of situations, and to have long discussions with some of them, especially with Ozaki himself. I have also taken advantage of the notes and reports, both published and private, of numerous others who have studied or stayed at Shinkyō—among them an American coed, an Israeli newsman, a Russian ethnographer, and an array of Japanese scholars and journalists.

To give an account of Shinkyō as a "total way of life" as ethnographers do for primitive tribes and peasant villagers, I would need much more time and much more information. My goal here is narrower: to use some materials from Shinkyō as a means to illuminate aspects of rural Japanese tradition and its re-formulation. For this I believe my materials suffice. If I do not have an intensive knowledge of the personalities and attitudes of all members (which could be gained by a longer stay), I do know enough to see beyond and behind the "official" presentation-of-self which they give the casual visitor and which Mrs. Sugihara exemplifies in some of her rationalizing paragraphs.

Outsiders sometimes describe Shinkyō as a collectivist movement or a utopian community. (I first learned of it from Japanese colleagues who knew I was studying utopian groups.) Insiders consider this wrong. From their point of view Shinkyō is a far-better-than-ordinary way of life, to be sure, and worth emulating. But it is not an "intentional community" or a "cause"; it simply happened to evolve as

Ozaki and the four families struggled to correct flaws they found in Tenri practice, in the Kasama power structure, and in Japanese rural custom.

Legally, in fact, Shinkyō is not a corporation or commune. The tatami-factory is registered and taxed as a business enterprise. But the community as such has no formal status; it is held together entirely by members' loyalties to each other and to Ozaki Sensei. The real property and motor vehicles which they use collectively remain severally registered in the names of the four families; the other members who joined after the war presumably have no ownership rights in them. If they chose, the four families could divide the property and go their separate ways. That they have not done so, that they continue to share with the other members, is a tribute to the "state of mind" that solidifies Shinkyō.

Shinkyō without Ozaki would be like *Hamlet* without Hamlet. It was born most immediately from his personal dilemmas; it thrives on his leadership and on members' loyalty to him; and many of its unique features derive from his inventiveness and powers of persuasion. As a commune it may very well not survive his demise, thus sharing the fate of vast numbers of communal groups throughout history. Ozaki himself professes to care only for the present, not for future generations—a stance that helped precipitate the nervous disorder which Mrs. Sugihara relates of herself in Chapter Eleven. A cynic might retort that since Ozaki has no living offspring he may also be less constrained than other men by thoughts of providing for heirs.

As a younger son, Ozaki had no claims, either by law or by custom, to his family's property. The postwar family law code prescribes equal shares for all offspring, although custom still favors inheritance by one child (ideally but not necessarily the eldest son). When Ozaki was a boy, however, both law and custom dictated that a younger son must leave the household and make his own way. Parents and kinsmen would try to help a younger son by arranging for him an apprenticeship or an adoption as heir to a sonless couple: both methods are exemplified in the case of Seki Noboru in Chapter Four. Or they would try to provide advanced schooling for the young man, as was done with Ozaki himself when he was sent to be trained for the Tenri ministry.

Ozaki says he enjoyed his first years in primary school and even dreamed of becoming a teacher. But when he was in fourth grade his father died, and after that the family could not afford to send any of its sons beyond the six years of school that then were compulsory. Ozaki began to skimp on his homework in order to spend most of his hours after school cutting straw for sandals and doing other family chores. I am not sure that he did this because the family was destitute, although that is the reason he gives today. The family may have suffered a setback, but it appears to have been moderately well off by Kasama standards. So I am inclined to ascribe his boyish diligence, and much of his life-long vigor for that matter, to a deep need to atone for feelings of guilt over the premature death of his parent. This is often cited as a feature of Japanese psychodynamics in general; we can see it in Ozaki in particular in his stress upon filiality and striving to repay obligations.

Such a generalized motivation can, of course, be manifested in many different ways. I do not presume to have deep insight into Ozaki's psyche; and I am suspicious of those psychoanalysts who, by cleverly twisting a few complexes, purport to account for much of a man's emotional dynamics. I merely wish to point up how themes of duty and repayment are central to major events in his life, how they appear in many aspects of his conduct, and how by his influence they color much of the Shinkyō way of life. The first of these themes involves an exact and literal reckoning of moral obligations, and a demand that they be fulfilled regardless of pain or cost. The second involves a tendency to

avoid such formal commitments (since they are so constrict-
ing), or to put it the other way a preference for informal
modes of interaction.

The insistence upon a balancing of moral accounts
comes out most obviously in the exact repayment of money
debts: Shinkyō people, Mrs. Sugihara tells us in Chapter
Ten, would starve themselves before they would fail to clear
away a loan by its due-date. She also describes how in 1941,
to save face for the mayor who had befriended them, they
bought a fire-pump and lent it to the township even though
this meant that they had to sell off two acres of paddy—a
step that most Japanese rice-farmers would regard as occupational treason.

This might seem like a rather exaggerated and almost
childishly naive sense of honesty. It should not, however, be
taken as an indication of some pathological sort of rigidity;
Ozaki is as mature and flexible as any man I have known.
The point is simply that like all mature men he has consistent styles of conduct, and one of these is a tendency to
be quite literal where most Japanese would be more meta-
phorical, in situations involving formal obligations. Seki
Noboru's apprenticeship is a good illustration—Ozaki insisting that the young man strip and be taken into the craftsman's house in his birthday suit. Another and less drastic
instance occurs fairly often. A visitor to Shinkyō may hand
Ozaki a *meishi*—the printed name-card that is so much a
part of Japanese good manners. When Ozaki accepts it saying, "But I have no card to give you," the visitor is likely to
reply politely, "Well, that is all right." Ozaki will fire back,
"Is it? Why is it all right for you to give me a card if I don't
give you one?" Or there is the well-known Japanese custom of deprecating the gifts one offers; commercial gift-
wrappings, for example, often are imprinted *sōhin*, "poor
goods." Once when Ozaki went to talk to a social club in a
nearby town, he was presented with an honorarium. The
money was properly wrapped in white paper, and inscribed

sun shi, "a trifle," or literally "an inch of paper." "What do you mean, 'an inch'?" said Ozaki, "Shouldn't you make it at least a foot?"

In some men this penchant for scrupulousness might result in proliferating defense mechanisms of a formal sort: rituals and ceremonies, creeds, uniforms, salutes and the like. Ozaki and Shinkyō have taken the opposite path; they are passionately informal. They have no written records or rules, official statements, or brochures. Ozaki says that he once began to keep a diary but soon quit because he felt it was making him more concerned with describing life than with living it. Although he enjoys talking about Shinkyō, he rarely will accept invitations to lecture about it publicly, and he resists recorded interviews. Mrs. Sugihara's book is, of course, an official description of sorts. But as she points out, she began it as an informal memorandum just for the members; it reached print only after a Sakurai acquaintance heard of it and suggested it to a Tokyo publisher.

There are no constitution or bylaws, no elected set of officers or formal meetings. Most decisions are reached by casual discussion in small groups at work or at meals or in the bath. Now and then members may be asked to linger in the dining room after a meal for a general discussion, but such sessions are not a matter of routine. There is a Shinkyō slogan—Nothing Is More Precious Than Harmony— and a Shinkyō anthem. But both were bestowed upon the group by visitors, and seem to be recited mainly for the benefit of visitors. Ozaki and his followers do not propagandize or attempt to enlarge the scope of the community; if they did expand it, almost certainly they would be forced to develop "secondary" and formalized roles and rules and means of social control.

So far, they have not even kept formal account books. The leaders have a general idea of income and outgo, savings and cash on hand. Mrs. Sugihara jots down rough notes on household expenses, and Yamanaka does likewise for the factory. But rather than reckon profits for tax purposes, Shinkyō simply hands over each year's sale-receipts to the tax office and pays whatever they levy. Members get no regular stipend or allowance, but they are free to take money from the petty cash box kept by the duty cook. Strong informal sanctions, loyalty, and an ample income combine to make the system workable. Cash and goods do sometimes "disappear," but the Shinkyō people would rather absorb an occasional loss this way than risk the haggling and bickering that would probably accompany a system of precise bookkeeping.

Overt signs of status are likewise at a minimum. All eat the same food and are free to help themselves at any time to snacks, beer, sake, and cigarettes. All have roughly equivalent clothing and living quarters; all go together on frequent short vacation trips. They address each other by diminutives or nicknames. Ozaki and the four families sometimes seem to fare slightly better—as, for example, when they were treated in 1965 to a jet vacation to Hong Kong and Taiwan. But in view of the fact that they also shoulder additional responsibilities as leaders, these differences scarcely appear unreasonable or exploitative, at least to an outsider.

Ozaki likes to inveigh against status inequalities, as in Chapter Eight when he asks the communist recruiter if the Party elite live the same kind of life as the rank-and-file. Earlier we hear him tell Seki Iwazō that a man should not rely upon status and power inherited from his father but should create his own, and furthermore should share the inheritance equally with his siblings. "Formal office, after all, constricts you," he said to me one day. "I found that one trouble with walking around in a priest's garments is that the faithful get upset if they see you taking a leak in public. Imagine what it is like being Emperor: he can't relieve himself like an ordinary man." There are no individual mortuary tablets at Shinkyō as in most Japanese dwellings, only a col-

Kotoe

lective gravestone. All goods are communal (except the legal registry of property mentioned earlier). And at times children have been sent to sleep in the rooms of adults other than their parents, as a way to weaken family ties. The years of being ostracized, of course, must have been a vivid lesson in the pains of being treated by formal categories.

The nearest thing to ritual in Shinkyō life is a daily rhythm of work and relaxation punctuated by collective bathing. Nemaki are the only "uniforms" bearing the Shinkyō imprint; and they are all in the style of the nemaki which resort hotels lend to guests. Not all members share Ozaki's near-compulsion for cleanliness; sometimes they tease him about it. But seldom does a member fail to bathe and don nemaki in the evening. This has a thoroughly practical component, to be sure. Tatami-making is dirty and tiresome work, as is the kind of farm labor that used to be

Shinkyō's mainstay. But visitors too, though they may arrive spotless, are soon urged to shuck their clothes and bathe away the dirt and strain of travel.

Ozaki has developed an idiom of bathing that pervades Shinkyō lifeways. The baths themselves are imposing; better ones exist only in exclusive inns or the homes of the very rich. The large communal bath can hold about forty people; and it has a great window overlooking the factory and the fields of Kasama. Members can loll in the bath as they watch these who once ostracized them now toiling in the fields. There are two smaller tubs elsewhere, one tiled and one of aromatic cypress, for those wanting a bit of privacy.

Bathing carries several implications in the Ozaki-Shinkyō view. Cleanliness naturally is one. "Nobody else in Japan loves farm life as much as I do," says Ozaki, "and nobody hates as much the filth that goes with it." If farm families would just get into the habit of bathing at the end of the day, remarks Mrs. Sugihara in her narrative, it would be a revolution. When groups of farm wives tour Shinkyō, Ozaki likes to taunt them both for their unclean habits and for their tendency to sit stiffly (and thus politely) as he talks to them. "Let us have a show of hands," he may say to them, "How many of you clean yourselves after you take a piss in the fields? There, you see! Filthy!"

Sexuality, though muted, is another bath feature. "After all," Ozaki may say to the women's groups, "who wants to go to bed with a smelly wife?" Mixed bathing is standard at Shinkyō—as it is not in many parts of Japan, other than within households or at resort hotels, American stereotypes to the contrary. "Where else can you bathe with scenery like this?" said one of the younger men to me in the tub one day. Then as he noticed that I was looking at the Kasama hills, he added, "No, no, I mean the scenery indoors." Ozaki and some of the members also believe, as do quite a few Japanese, that mixed bathing is healthful because it diffuses hormones from each sex to the other, and from young to old.

Collective bathing also means togetherness. One melts into the group spirit as into the shared steaming pool. Ozaki

Kotoè

says, "The secret of communal life is not to leave the bath-water dirty for those who enter after you." In a slight exaggeration, collective bathing might even be called the Shin-kyō equivalent of holy communion—note that Ozaki made kindling of the Kasama Chapel altar and used it to fire up a bath in which the four families then took part. "From the dirtiest thing in the community comes the purest," he said to me one day. "Every day we feed dusty straw waste into that black furnace, and out comes the evening's pure boiling water."

Lastly, the bath serves as a transition-marker between daily toil and daily ease. Ozaki likes to explain it with a larva-and-butterfly image. "By day we are grubby worms spinning away; then we soak off the cocoon and emerge as evening butterflies. When I get into that bath, my cares all melt away. Religion and philosophy are supposed to give you a sense of security. I get it by working hard all day and then scrubbing off the tension at night and being completely relaxed until next morning. Isn't that better than praying and fasting and meditating?" This sense, that the true nature of being and of life are to be found right within one's daily round of life, is a common feature in much of the Japanese philosophical tradition; but Ozaki has managed to give it his own unique mode of expression.

But Shinkyō is not just a product of Ozaki's personality; it is the outcome of several processes of interaction. Ozaki's estrangement from Tenri led to a strengthening of his bonds with the four families. This in turn brought on enmity with the Seki faction, ostracism, and eventually the move to Manchuria. Finally, Japan's defeat in the war brought a return to Kasama, and a more supportive environment in which the commune expanded and then attained wealth and power.

Shinkyō could be called a Tenri way of life purged of Tenri's mysteries and formalities. Ozaki says that his outlook today does not differ markedly from that he held as a Tenri missionary, except that he sees no value in prayers or altars or religious bureaucracies. Such things, Mrs. Sugihara tells us in Chapter Two, can actually hinder one from attaining a faith in things-as-they-are. But the Shinkyō themes of cleanliness and of striving to repay obligations echo dominant Tenri concerns.

In Tenri parlance the ills and misfortunes of life are due to *hokori*—"dust" or "dirt." It is sin, in a sense, though without Christian connotations of radical and inherent evil. We accumulate dirt by our misuse of the self, which has merely been lent to us by the gods, to whom we are thereby in debt. Dirty selves upset the harmony that can and should exist among self, society, and the universe. To bring it about we must cleanse away our hokori. In the words of the opening line of the *Mikagura Uta*, the "Dancing Psalm" that is Tenri's most sacred song, "Cleanse us of all evil and save us, oh parent god of divine wisdom." [Tenri = "divine wisdom" or "heavenly principles."] Tenri buildings and officials are noted for their cleanliness; the sacred precincts in Tenri City are swept twice daily, and those who guard its most sacred altar provide the spirit of the sect's foundress with not only three meals but also a hot bath.

There are eight types of hokori: greed, stinginess, partiality, hatred, animosity, anger, covetousness, and arrogance. Mrs. Sugihara's narrative tacitly furnishes examples of how Ozaki Sensei avoids all of these; at times when she recounts his virtues the book reads almost like hagiography. Stinginess, for example, includes reluctance to pay taxes or perform public service, or return anything borrowed, or to lend to those in need. Mrs. Sugihara tells how the four families, though ostracized and scorned, went on performing their patriotic duty as citizens helping to send off recruits. She also mentions road and riverbank repairs, school land, an electric power line, imperial shrines, and other public services which Shinkyō has sponsored. At times she hints that Shinkyō was tricked into it by Seki's scheming; at times she suggests that it came out of motives of pure generosity. Ozaki is less naive; he recognizes that often enough his main purpose was to make Seki lose face in front

179

of the villagers. "Conspicuous contribution" seems to be as much a feature of rural life in Japan as conspicuous consumption. However, Shinkyō's generosity extends beyond the arena of Kasama in-fighting. About half of the present members are once-destitute people who have been taken in since the end of the war. And from time to time still others are admitted, although there is no intention of expanding the scale of operations. (Ozaki receives an average of about three letters a day from people all over Japan who want to be taken in, most of them destitute or in distress; his usual reply urges them to strive harder where they are.) Furthermore, for several years Shinkyō has cared for two or three juvenile parolees at a time, and in 1967 it built and began supporting a center for the training of some fifty retarded children.

Ozaki's break with Tenri no doubt stems from multiple causes, as Mrs. Sugihara indicates: marital difficulties, an incurably ill child, a desire to return to Kasama and to farming. But he justifies it on grounds that Tenri's gods and ministers have failed to meet their obligations. He does not atheistically deny that gods exist; the trouble is that they are not rewarding their children's devotion with health and security, much less joyous living and cosmic harmony. Likewise the priests, who profess to serve the children but also fatten their pockets with contributions the children bring to the gods. The point is a sore and delicate one for Tenri, as for many religious organizations. One official Tenri explanation stresses the difference between charity and progressive service. The former is between man and man, the latter between man and the gods. Since the self is but a loan from the gods, if a man will return it—renounce selfish interests and entrust himself to the gods—he will actually gain great powers and be capable of amazing charity. Foundress Nakayama Miki once demonstrated her renunciation by distributing all of her family's goods to the poor around her. Zealous believers often want to follow her personal example, and then must be persuaded instead to give their goods to the church. Even Tenri believers like to burlesque the opening line of the Dancing Psalm, converting it to "Clear away our homes and sell our paddies, oh parent god of divine wisdom." (*Ashiki o harōte tasuketamae* becomes *Yashiki o harōte ta-uri tamae*). So from his point of view Ozaki was quite consistent when he told the Special High Police Chief that he had not left Tenri, it had left him.

Many another man might have been content, his dilemmas resolved, once he had resigned his post. Ozaki says he did feel a great relief as soon as he shed his Tenri robes and became an "ordinary" man again. He calls it the first of his two great rebirths (the second being his release from jail in 1945 when he again became "ordinary"). But Ozaki is extra-ordinary in having the attributes of a good moral entrepreneur: confidence, courage, and an ability to turn personal problems into public issues. With these attributes he won the support of the four families; with them he went on to create the fabric of mutual reliance that has given Shinkyō its remarkable combination of adaptability and staying power. He relies upon the others to advise and consent; they rely upon him not just as their supervisor but as their sensei.

As I pointed out in the Foreword, the term sensei is applied to a variety of roles, but in all cases with the implication that this is a person who is trustworthy and "responsible." A true sensei, as Mrs. Sugihara says of Ozaki, is a "spiritual pillar." He is also a moral entrepreneur. I mean that a sensei may not be adept at combining material factors of production, selling his goods and "meeting a payroll." But he is adept at combining emotional and symbolic resources, and repaying his followers with a sense of security or perhaps what the existentialists call "authenticity."

This is what prompted me to choose *Sensei And His People* as a title, because Ozaki and Shinkyō exemplify a mode of human relationships that I think most Japanese value highly, long for, and reach out for. It is sometimes referred to as a feeling of ultimate confidence in a limited human nexus—in contrast to, say, ultimate trust in an impersonal God or in an abstract framework of Law (whether natural or man-made), as seems more characteristic in the West. Members of such a nexus do not become slavish puppets to their sensei. But they do seem to accept his decisions (see Chapter Eight) with about as little doubt and fear as is possible given the manifold uncertainties of human affairs. His personal presence, as a known human quantity, furnishes a living guarantee that their course of action is not merely desirable but absolutely *right*.

This often disturbs the Western observer, to whom it appears at best dangerously inconsistent and at worst downright irrational. True, it may not provide the kind of doctrinal continuity that the Western intellectual observer prizes; but what it can provide is a continuity of personal ties that validate the correctness of the group's actions. Note that in Zen and many other strands in Japanese religion and ethics there is unusual stress upon having a sensei who personally was trained by a man who in turn was personally trained by another, etc., in a direct and unbroken chain back to the founder of the sect. Or similarly, the patriotic insistence that unlike all other royal pedigrees the Imperial Japanese family line reaches down in unbroken continuity from the Sun Goddess to the incumbent Emperor.

The Shinkyō name also needs to be understood in this light. I have translated it as "state of mind"; even this betrays a mentalistic and cognitive Western bias. The *shin* of shinkyō encompasses the anatomical and emotional heart as well as the mind; or emotion and affect and feeling as well as thought. The common word shinkyō thus denotes some sort of attitude or stance toward life—in the case of Shinkyō primarily an attitude of reliance upon the group nexus and its sensei—but one that cannot easily be reduced to a list of tenets. A homophone shinkyō (which would not be confused in writing because two entirely different Chinese graphs are used) does, however, mean "new doctrines," which is at the root of Chief Yoshimura's confusion about Ozaki and the group (see Chapter Four).

I find it difficult to characterize the Shinkyō state of mind in positive terms, beyond the idea of solidarity authenticated by a living sensei. In this regard Shinkyō is more a manifestation of, than a reaction against, general Japanese values and preferred behavior patterns. Historically, on the other hand, it took shape as a set of reactions: first against Tenri formalism, then against village bossism and social exclusiveness. In time the group came to embrace practices and principles of collective living, and members now advocate them, although in a passive manner. But collective living itself has been somewhat incidental to the main purpose, which has been to sustain the "state of mind" which developed among Ozaki and the four families.

A further factor has helped. Ozaki and the heads of the four families were, after all, linked by previous ties of kinship and neighborliness and village co-residence. They came together as age-mates, with the ease of communication and the shared outlook that only age-mates can have. It may not be impossible to build a viable commune with a random group of strangers of different ages and backgrounds —human nature seems to be such that even a random assembly quickly generates a modicum of shared understandings. But having a cadre of age-mates certainly gave Shinkyō a head start.

In another environment Ozaki and the four families might simply have become church drop-outs. But as they banded together they also came to share Ozaki's resentment towards Seki and his bossiness—a resentment that probably had been smouldering in each of them individually for some time. Factional enmity is endemic in Japanese villages;

elsewhere the four families might have been able to compromise with Seki (the narrative hints of attempts to do so) or strike a cold-war balance of powers. But in Kasama and environs the majority of people are Tenri supporters. Thus on the one hand the dramatic and drastic act of altar-smashing became an issue of widespread concern in the area, not just a gossip-worthy wrangle in some little church. And on the other hand Ozaki's intransigence about Tenri, and the four families' vow to support him "even if it kills us" converted the factional differences with Seki into differences over *ends* and not just means. The dispute began to take on public, even cosmic, overtones. Or if that sounds overstated, at the very least it was a visible smudge upon the facade of village harmony.

I am not suggesting that ostracism was inevitable, but given the situation it was no surprise. Ostracism has been a time-favored method for dealing with village recalcitrants in Japan. The folk term for it is *mura-hachibu*, or "village eight-parts." Folk theory says that village social interaction comprises ten parts. Lists of the ten vary from region to region, but by and large they include such things as rights to use communal irrigation facilities and communal forest lands, disaster relief, aid at weddings and wakes, and so on down to everyday friendliness. When a family is ostracized it is supposed to be deprived of eight of the ten parts. To have them restored, the head of the household must repent (whether or not he personally committed the offense), make appropriate restitution, and persuade a village influential to stand as guarantor. Since World War II the courts have held ostracism illegal. But cases still come to light, and many others probably never are reported. These days ostracism is blunted as a sanction. Materially, most farmers use commercial fertilizers and power machinery, and so are not greatly dependent upon green manure from village common lands or exchange labor from their neighbors. And psychologically, the modern mass communications media and relatively easy transportation allow a villager to escape the near-total isolation that ostracism might once have imposed. Nevertheless, even today most families fear the humiliation and nuisance-value of being ostracized, and are concerned lest it happen.

Usually an ostracism falls upon a single family, which either repents or leaves the community. Here it fell upon four at once. All of them were what the Maoists call "middle peasants," families with enough economic resources to get by on their own, as shown by the speed with which they went out and bought their own thresher and huller when they were refused use of the community-owned ones. A further example was their ability to put together funds for new buildings and for donating the shrines, at a very real sacrifice to be sure but without bankrupting themselves. The ostracism gave them a powerful common cause; the emergence of their own collective settlement gave them new goals to fight for. Also, the fact that they were age-mates in their early maturity, and that some of their parents refused to join the collective or even condone it, helped by lessening their loyalties to family continuity and family independence.

That Shinkyō was rebuilt in Kasama after 1945 probably was due to a lack of alternatives more than to anything else. Ozaki says that they simply were driven back upon the resources that they still held. But as the tatami trade became profitable, they also began to gain power over Kasama, and today it is dependent upon them. The motives here are complex. In part there has been a desire for retribution; however, it has not been retribution of a directly punitive sort but of a shaming brought upon the rest of the village by Shinkyō's many conspicuous contributions to the general welfare. In part there are emotional ties to birthplace, kin, and friends, although complicated by the ostracism and the suffering it brought. And in part there is Ozaki's moral entrepreneurship, which reaches out only indirectly to wider segments of Japanese society but which he funnels directly into Kasama.

I have already said that he does not intend to expand Shinkyō by recruiting outsiders. However, he does dream of merging Shinkyō and Kasama into a village-wide commune. Then, he says, it might truly serve as a model for Japanese rural reconstruction. Some of the villagers could continue to grow rice and vegetables, as they do now. Others could be taken into the tatami enterprise—Mrs. Sugihara to the contrary, the shop does hire a few Kasama men as tatami finishers and as truck drivers. The factory has also been, for more than a decade now, a ready market for all surplus straw from Kasama farms (and for that matter, most other farms in a dozen-mile radius). The villagers might continue to live in their present homes if they wished, or move to modern and efficient apartment quarters like those which Shinkyō people already inhabit. In either case communal kitchens, workshops—and of course baths— would be constructed. And other sources of income would be developed, so that all Kasama could enjoy the urban middle-class standard of living which Shinkyō already has.

Ozaki envisions creating a Kasama complex that would combine dairying and tourism. A herd of about four hundred milch cows would be pastured in the hills south of the village, and tended by a few well-trained dairymen. The milk and meat would provide one source of income. There would also be facilities to which city tourists could come to picnic and relax—and buy genuine fresh milk taken directly from its bovine source. A resort hotel would be built, one having a fine set of baths like Shinkyō's, overlooking the scenery. Perhaps a heart-shaped bath of red tiles, or a real milk bath.

Informally and in his own style of gentle persuasion, Ozaki keeps after village influentials to join him in the venture. "After all," he said to me one day, "we sort of owe it to the village: if it hadn't been for the ostracism, we would not have discovered the power of this way of life we have. Besides, show me a 'utopian' group that gives a damn about its neighbors."

More and more, as the last remark shows, Ozaki and the people of Shinkyō find themselves responding to images cast upon them by their Japanese countrymen at large. Letters of inquiry come daily; and almost daily there come inquiring students, scholars, journalists, administrators, politicians, or whole busloads of the merely curious. I said that Shinkyō does not proselytize or even propagandize; you could say that it doesn't need to, since the world now comes to its door to learn what it has to teach about the building of islands of collective social security in the anomic sea that is modern industrial civilization. Ozaki, the four families, and the rest of the Shinkyō people have, from their point of view, simply been "doing their own thing"; they have not been trying to furnish Japan with a communitarian model for reconciling the agrarian past with the industrial future. That, however, is part of their present fate. Such are the ironies of human action.